Professor Dunn writes: 'Paul's lett_ _ _one of the fiercest and most pole_ _ _Bible. That is what makes it such an_ _ _deal with. For it comes from the _ _ _ _ _ _ _ _ _ _g of a vigorous new movement (Christianity), when basic principles were first being formulated, and when the whole character of the movement was at stake. In the pages of Galatians we can actually witness fundamental features of Christian theology taking shape. It is a cry from the heart of one at the very front of the line of Christian advance dealing with questions which determined the identity and whole life-style of those to whom he wrote. Here readers can little doubt that they are encountering the living heart of Paul's gospel. There is an elemental quality about it, to which those tired of compromising half truths are drawn when they feel the instinctive impulse to return to first principles. This study, which reflects the new perspective on Paul, helps to explain more clearly than hitherto both the issues which confronted Paul and the powerful theological arguments he brought to bear in response, and so brings fresh illumination to a document still capable of shaping both lives and theology today.'

Palms Presbyterian Church
Adult Library
3410 South Third Street
Jacksonville Beach, FL 32250

NEW TESTAMENT THEOLOGY

General Editor: James D. G. Dunn,
Lightfoot Professor of Divinity, University of Durham

The theology of Paul's Letter to the Galatians

This series provides a programmatic survey of the individual writings of the New Testament. It aims to remedy the deficiency of available published material, which has tended to concentrate on historical, textual, grammatical, and literary issues at the expense of the theology, or to lose distinctive emphases of individual writings in systematised studies of 'The Theology of Paul' and the like. New Testament specialists here write at greater length than is usually possible in the introductions to commentaries or as part of other New Testament theologies, and explore the theological themes and issues of their chosen books without being tied to a commentary format, or to a thematic structure drawn from elsewhere. When complete, the series will cover all the New Testament writings, and will thus provide an attractive, and timely, range of texts around which courses can be developed.

THE THEOLOGY OF
PAUL'S LETTER TO
THE GALATIANS

JAMES D. G. DUNN

Lightfoot Professor of Divinity, University of Durham

CAMBRIDGE
UNIVERSITY PRESS

Published by the Press Syndicate of the University of Cambridge
The Pitt Building, Trumpington Street, Cambridge CB2 1RP
40 West 20th Street, New York, NY 10011–4211, USA
10 Stamford Road, Oakleigh, Melbourne 3166, Australia

© Cambridge University Press 1993

First published 1993

Printed in Great Britain at the University Press, Cambridge

A catalogue record for this book is available from the British Library

Library of Congress cataloguing in publication data
Dunn, James D. G., 1939–
The theology of Paul's Letter to the Galatians / James D. Dunn.
p.   cm. – (New Testament theology)
Includes bibliographical references and indexes.
ISBN 0 521 35127 8 (hardback) – ISBN 0 521 35953 8 (paperback)
1. Bible. N.T. Galatians – Theology. I. Title. II Series.
BS2685.5.D87   1993
227'.406 – dc20   93–9 CIP

ISBN 0 521 35127 8 hardback
ISBN 0 521 35953 8 paperback

To
PETER STUHLMACHER
fellow student
at the feet of
Paul the theologian

Contents

Editor's preface

Although the New Testament is usually taught within Departments or Schools or Faculties of Theology/Divinity/Religion, theological study of the individual New Testament writings is often minimal or at best patchy. The reasons for this are not hard to discern.

For one thing, the traditional style of studying a New Testament document is by means of straight exegesis, often verse by verse. Theological concerns jostle with interesting historical, textual, grammatical and literary issues, often at the cost of the theological. Such exegesis is usually very time-consuming, so that only one or two key writings can be treated in any depth within a crowded three-year syllabus.

For another, there is a marked lack of suitable textbooks round which courses could be developed. Commentaries are likely to lose theological comment within a mass of other detail in the same way as exegetical lectures. The section on the theology of a document in the Introduction to a commentary is often very brief and may do little more than pick out elements within the writing under a sequence of headings drawn from systematic theology. Excursuses usually deal with only one or two selected topics. Likewise larger works on New Testament Theology usually treat Paul's letters as a whole and, having devoted the great bulk of their space to Jesus, Paul and John, can spare only a few pages for others.

In consequence, there is little incentive on the part of teacher or student to engage with a particular New Testament document, and students have to be content with a general overview, at best complemented by in-depth study of (parts of) two or three New Testament writings. A serious corollary to this is the degree to which students are thereby incapacitated in the task of integrating their New Testament study with the rest of their Theology or Religion courses, since often they are capable only of drawing on the general overview or on a sequence of particular verses treated atomistically. The growing importance of a literary-critical approach to individual documents simply highlights the present deficiencies even more. Having been given little experience in handling individual New Testament writings as such at a theological level, most students are very ill-prepared to develop a properly integrated literary and theological response to particular texts. Ordinands too need more help than they currently receive from textbooks, so that their preaching from particular passages may be better informed theologically.

There is need therefore for a series to bridge the gap between too brief an introduction and too full a commentary where theological discussion is lost among too many other concerns. It is our aim to provide such a series. That is, a series where New Testament specialists are able to write at a greater length on the theology of individual writings than is usually possible in the introductions to commentaries or as part of New Testament Theologies, and to explore the theological themes and issues of these writings without being tied to a commentary format or to a thematic structure provided from elsewhere. The volumes seek both to describe each document's theology, and to engage theologically with it, noting also its canonical context and any specific influence it may have had on the history of Christian faith and life. They are directed at those who already have one or two years of full-time New Testament and theological study behind them.

University of Durham   JAMES D. G. DUNN

Preface

Anyone who is interested in the doing and making of theology could hardly find a better starting place than the letter of Paul to the Galatians. For here is Christianity's first great theologian – arguably its greatest theologian – in full flood. Here we can never lose the sense that issues of profound significance are in the balance, to be argued for and defended as though life itself was at stake – as, for Paul, it was. Here we see Christian theology in the making, 'the truth of the gospel' being formulated in its innermost heart and immediate corollaries – at least as Paul saw it. Even if the task of the twentieth-century commentator were to be confined to merely offering a historical description of the theology which Paul here unfolds, it would be hard to avoid being caught up in the issues of first principles, essentials and priorities, hard to remain untouched by the intensity with which Paul engages in the argument. And for those who wish to engage in the theological debate with Paul for themselves, to treat Galatians as a dialogue partner, the power and the passion of the letter can at times be almost overwhelming.

The writing of the following pages has therefore been a labour of love. The sense of engaging with a profound, if somewhat irascible theologian has never left me. As my appreciation for the thrust of the argument, for the allusions, nuances and overtones grew, so my admiration for the man and his theology has steadily deepened. If then the present volume contributes even a little to a fresh and fuller understanding of Paul's theology and Paul's gospel the labour will have been repaid in sufficient measure.

Although I was concerned primarily with the theology of Galatians it was clear to me from the start that the theological argumentation had to be set in its historical context. In a day when many question the need or value of doing so in handling a text like Galatians, my own conviction has been repeatedly reinforced that this letter cannot be adequately understood except in relation to the situation to which it was addressed. For this is no ivory tower theology, no theology in the abstract, but theology in vigorous and outspoken dialogue with all too real and specific situations. It is true that we cannot hear the other side of the dialogue in its own terms, but the alternatives and threats as seen by Paul are clear enough. For those who wish then either to appreciate Paul's grasp of the gospel or to engage with him in assessing and expressing claims to theological truth, it simply will not do to abstract the words of Galatians from their context in the letter or from the letter's context in history. For it is the contingency, the context-relatedness of Paul's statements which both gave and still give them their point; a restatement of the same truth in a different or later context requires a different formulation. The Paul of 1 Cor. 9.19–23 would have been the first to see that. Any use of Galatians in doing theology which ignores the historical contextuality of Paul's statements in Galatians, therefore, is almost bound to misperceive particular points in the argument and to lose the balance of the whole. To hear Paul in his historical context is to recognize more clearly not only *why* he says what he says, but also *what* it is he actually is saying in the letter.

This study comes at the end of a sustained interaction with Galatians stretching over twelve or so years. During the first part of that period my main concern was with Paul's letter to the Romans; from the first it was clear to me that the latter could not be adequately understood without constant recourse to the former – another indication of Galatians' importance. But since 1988 Galatians itself has been my principal concern, particularly in writing a commentary on the letter for the Black's New Testament Commentary series. Having worked through the text of the letter in close detail it was a particular pleasure to be able to take a step backwards and to write a theological overview of the whole document. Since space did not permit a section on the theology of the letter in the introduction to the commentary, the two volumes overlap to a surprisingly small extent and can be regarded as companion volumes.

My thanks are due to Alex Wright, Cambridge University Press's editor for the series, whose support for the series and encouragement in the writing of this volume has made the venture still the more pleasurable. Regular participation in the Pauline Theology Group which has met annually for the past few years at the Society of Biblical Literature conferences has been a constant stimulus and delight, as also the more continuous dialogue with my colleagues and postgraduates at Durham. The volume is dedicated to Peter Stuhlmacher in celebration of our continuing Durham–Tübingen theological dialogue, not least on what the theology of Paul is for today. As for Meta, whose praise is far beyond rubies, she still can't quite believe that this volume was completed so quickly!

Abbreviations

ABD	*The Anchor Bible Dictionary*
BAGD	W. Bauer, *A Greek-English Lexicon of the New Testament and Other Early Christian Literature*, ed. W. F. Arndt and F. W. Gingrich; 2nd edition revised F. W. Gingrich & F. W. Danker
BJRL	*Bulletin of the John Rylands Library of Manchester*
CBQ	*Catholic Biblical Quarterly*
DSS	Dead Sea Scrolls
ER	*Epworth Review*
HTKNT	Herders theologischer Kommentar zum Neuen Testament
ICC	International Critical Commentary
IDB	*Interpreter's Dictionary of the Bible*, ed. G. A. Buttrick
JBL	*Journal of Biblical Literature*
JSNT	*Journal for the Study of the New Testament*
JSNTS	*JSNT* Supplement series
JTS	*Journal of Theological Studies*
KEK	Kritisch-exegetischer Kommentar über das Neue Testament
LSJ	H. G. Liddell and R. Scott, *A Greek-English Lexicon*, revised H. S. Jones
LXX	Septuagint = Greek version of Old Testament
NEB	New English Bible
NIGTC	New International Greek Testament Commentary
NIV	New International Version
NJB	New Jerusalem Bible

Abbreviations

NovT	*Novum Testamentum*
NRSV	New Revised Standard Version
NTS	*New Testament Studies*
par(s).	parallel(s)
REB	Revised English Bible
SBLDS	Society of Biblical Literature Dissertation Series
SEA	*Svensk Exegetisk Årsbok*
SJT	*Scottish Journal of Theology*
SNT	Supplement to *NovT*
SNTSMS	Society for New Testament Studies Monograph Series
TDNT	*Theological Dictionary of the New Testament*, ed. G. Kittell & G. Friedrich
WBC	Word Biblical Commentary
WUNT	Wissenschaftliche Untersuchungen zum Neuen Testament

CHAPTER I

Introduction

Paul's letter to the Galatians is one of the fiercest and most polemical writings in the Bible. It begins with a denunciation of those to whom it was written and of unnamed troublemakers (1.6–9). It dismisses another group of Christians as 'false brothers', makes snide remarks about the leaders of the Jerusalem church (2.6) and accuses Peter of hypocrisy and deceit (2.13–14). After two somewhat more restrained chapters, the tone of urgent pleading and denunciation is resumed (5.2–4, 7–10), including a rather crude and blackly humorous aside (5.12). And the final paragraph cannot resist a parting swipe at those behind the problems and challenges which the letter seeks to address (6.12–13).

It is this feature which makes Paul's letter such an exciting document to deal with. For Galatians is not an academic treatise drawn up in the calm autumn of a long life, the mature fruit of long debate, with every statement duly weighed and every phrase finely polished. Rather, it comes from the early morning of a vigorous new movement (Christianity), when basic principles were first being formulated, and when the whole character of the movement was at stake. In the pages of Galatians, one of the earliest documents in the New Testament, we see, as it were, fundamental features of Christian theology taking shape before our eyes. In no sense is Galatians an ivory tower tract remote from real life, the dispassionate statement of one high above the battle. Rather, it is a cry from the heart of one at the very front of the line of Christian advance, dealing with questions which determined the identity and whole life-style of those to whom he wrote. It is theology engaging with the challenge of competing interpretations of central beliefs and with the crisis of new adherents caught in the crossfire of whom to believe and how to act. It is itself theology under fire, theology in the midst, living theology. There can be no question that the man who wrote this letter was deeply engaged with and totally committed to what he wrote.

The same feature lies also, presumably, at the heart of the letter's influence in Christian history and theology. For the uninhibited nature of Paul's language gives the reader a unique insight into the heart of his theology. Here sentences carefully constructed to conceal more than they reveal, the ambiguous formulations of ecclesiastical compromise, are notable by their absence (2.6–10 may be an exception). Paul evidently wanted his Galatian audiences to be in no doubt as to where he stood, how he conceived the gospel, and what its consequences are. Here subsequent readers readily feel that they are encountering the living heart of Paul's gospel, stripped even of the qualifications and more measured tones of his subsequent letter to the Romans. This is theology in the raw, red-blooded theology, quintessential paulinism. There is an elemental quality about it, to which those tired of compromising half-truths are drawn when they feel the instinctive impulse to return to first principles. There is more nuclear power in these few pages than in the polemical cannons and mortars of theological treatises, twenty, fifty or one hundred times larger, which have peppered the history of Christianity.

Those who wish truly to engage in this letter and its theology must therefore be prepared themselves to engage in the process of theology: to ask why it was that Paul felt these points of theological principle so passionately; whether he was right in his conviction that there could be no 'other gospel' (1.7), other than what he preached, or whether, alternatively, his understanding and expression of the gospel were as unbalanced as those he attacked; and whether his gospel and its outworkings still provide a pattern for later generations and for today. Certainly as a model of theological integrity, where life-forming principles deeply felt are brought to clear expression, where contemporary questions and challenges are addressed boldly and directly, and where passionate conviction and theological sophistication are blended in powerful exposition, Galatians has few equals.

SETTING THE LETTER IN CONTEXT

In the case of a document so thoroughly related to a particular context in history, it is naturally important to try to locate that document as fully as possible in that context. Who were the 'foolish Galatians' (3.1)? What was the nature of the crisis which the letter writer was so worked up about? Why was he so worked up about it? Even before studying the letter in detail, the presumption must be strong that it will contain allusions and references to that context. And almost certainly some at least of these references and allusions will be so integrally related to the situation addressed, that they cannot be adequately understood without reference to that context.

This is where the task of interpreting a letter is bound to differ from the task of interpreting a narrative or treatise, where the author as author has stepped back from immediate involvement with the affairs of every day or of particular situations. A letter, more or less by definition, is part of a dialogue (between specific writer and specific recipients), and to abstract it from that dialogue is to lose something of its quality as answer to actual questions or propositions posed, and as questions or propositions requiring in turn an answer from actual recipients. And this letter of all letters is so much the voice of one man addressing a particular situation with urgency and passion that the task of setting it in context has an inescapable imperative.

This is not to say that a complete reconstruction of the historical context is possible. Nor to admit that, a complete reconstruction being impossible, much or most of the dialogic meaning of the letter's content will escape us. There are sufficient indications in the letter itself, especially when set against the larger context of the Judaism and Hellenistic world of the time, to enable us to reconstruct a fairly good picture of the situation in Galatia.[1] There will, of course, be nuances and allusions which are difficult to recognize and will be missed, because our knowledge of the context is so sketchy. And we will frequently be unsure of the extent to which we should discount the bias and one-sidedness of Paul's own view of the issues. But even so we can reconstruct in sufficient detail both the chain of events leading up to the letter (thanks above all to Paul's own autobiographical account in chapters 1 and 2), and the theological views which Paul opposes in the letter, to be reasonably confident of recognizing the primary thrust of most of what Paul says.

This stress on the meaning of the letter within the historical context within which and for which it was written is also not intended to exclude the possibility and legitimacy of other readings of the text in later and different contexts. We will take note of some of these in the final chapter. But a text which is treated as endlessly flexible and capable of multiple contradictory readings either becomes a mere tool of dogma and ideology, or a reflex of unconstrained egoistic pluralism. In fact, however, the language of the text itself provides all the constraints necessary, especially when we recall that it was written in Greek, and that therefore understanding of it is from the start dependent on a knowledge of Greek terms, syntax and idiom at a particular period in history. In my own view, the text set within context, particularly in the case of a letter and especially in the case of this letter, determines a limited range of understanding of the text, in large themes certainly, but also in many particulars, which is bound to be normative for all other readings.[2]

The author

Unlike many ancient documents whose authors we can only guess at, we know well who wrote Galatians. It was Paul – the

[1] See particularly J. M. G. Barclay, 'Mirror-Reading a Polemical Letter. Galatians as a Test Case', *JSNT* 31 (1987) pp. 73–93.
[2] For full discussion of the hermeneutical issues see particularly A. C. Thiselton, *New Horizons in Hermeneutics* (London: Harper Collins, 1992); see also my 'A Word in Time: Understanding the Bible Today', *ER* 19 (1992) pp. 27–42.

Paul who introduces himself in 1.1. Here at once we discover the first of Galatians' treasures. For Galatians provides us with more personal and autobiographical information than any of Paul's other letters, particularly in chapters 1 and 2. He starts at once by impressing his readers with his self-understanding as 'apostle' (1.1). We learn of his 'earlier life in Judaism' as a zealous Jew and persecutor of 'the church of God' (1.13–14). He tells us of his entry into Christian faith – his conversion as it is usually called (1.15–16). He relates his previous encounters with the Christian leadership in Jerusalem (2.1–10) and what appears to have been a highly contentious confrontation with Peter in Antioch (2.11–14). He also gives some very personal reminiscences of his evangelizing visit to Galatia (4.12–20) and hints at the personal, physical cost of his strenuous life (6.17). When all this is integrated with the teaching of the letter itself, it enables us to build up a strong picture of Paul the missionary and theologian, and enables us to situate the letter to Galatia itself within both his life and his theology.

However, we should not simply abstract such information from the letter and be content to use it to construct a biographical profile. For the information is part of the letter. It serves the purpose of the letter. As recent rhetorical analysis of the letter had indicated, the autobiographical narrative in chapters 1 and 2 was intended to build up to and to introduce the principal theological argument of the following chapters.[3] The highly personal language of 2.14–21 and 6.11–17 is indication in itself of the degree to which Paul saw his own experience as an epitome of the gospel. It will be necessary, therefore, to look at this information in more detail in due course, since Paul's selection of autobiographical data and the way he uses it is itself part of the theology of the letter. As G. Lyons has observed, Paul 'presents his "autobiography" as a paradigm of the gospel of Christian freedom ... (and) considers himself in some sense a representative or even an embodiment

---

[3] H. D. Betz, *Galatians* (Hermeneia; Philadelphia: Fortress Press, 1979), pp. 58–62. See also below p. 15 and n. 26.

of that gospel'.[4] Whether this involved a degree of 'auto-biographical reconstruction', that is, personal reminiscences tailored to fit a subsequent perspective,[5] is something we will have to bear in mind. Such reflections also suggest a danger in assuming that the information provided by Paul will be 'pure' because first-hand, over against more 'tainted', second-hand information given by Acts. But since our concern is primarily with the theology of Galatians we need not pursue that issue further.

The recipients

Paul's reminiscences also provide valuable information about those to whom the letter was addressed and about their entry into Christian faith. They were Galatians (1.2; 3.1); that this means also that they were Gentiles is the clear implication of 4.8 ('you did not know God and were in slavery to beings that by nature are no gods'). They had welcomed Paul's arrival with great warmth and solicitousness for his poor physical condition (4.13–15). To them Paul had preached Christ cruci-fied (3.1) and their response of faith had resulted in rich and powerful experiences of the Spirit (3.2–5). Here again, apart from their name and ethnic identity ('Galatians'), the infor-mation all serves Paul's theological purpose in writing the letter and we shall have to study it also with greater care if we are fully to appreciate that theology.

The main bone of contention for historical scholarship at this point has been the identity of the 'Galatians'. It is clear enough that they belonged to the region known by that name (Galatia), located in the heartland of Asia Minor (modern Turkey).[6] But was the name being used in an ethnic sense

---

[4] G. Lyons, *Pauline Autobiography. Towards a New Understanding* (SBLDS 73; Atlanta; Scholars Press, 1985), p. 171; see also J. H. Schütz, *Paul and the Anatomy of Apostolic Authority* (SNTSMS 26; Cambridge University Press, 1975) ch. 5; B. R. Gaventa, 'Galatians 1 and 2: Autobiography as Paradigm', *NovT* 28 (1986), pp. 309–26.

[5] As argued e.g. by N. Taylor, *Paul, Antioch and Jerusalem. A Study in Relationships and Authority in Earliest Christianity* (JSNTS 66; Sheffield Academic Press, 1992), pp. 155–70.

[6] The name derives from the Gallic tribes (the Gauls or Celts) who migrated into Asia Minor and settled in the region in the third century BC.

(Galatians = descendants of the original Gallic/Celtic settlers), or in an administrative sense (the Roman province of Galatia extended further south)? In fact the question has to do more with integrating the information provided by Galatians (the letter) into the programme of Paul's missionary work as recorded in Acts. For if the name was being used of the administrative territory, the Galatians in question could be citizens of the more cultured cities in the south of the region, the cities which, according to Acts 13–14, Paul visited during his 'first missionary journey' (Antioch, Iconium, Lystra and Derbe). Whereas, again according to Acts, Paul did not visit ethnic Galatia till what is usually incorrectly described as Paul's 'second missionary journey' (Acts 16.6). However, here again the issue has very little effect on the theology of the letter, except as it bears upon the relative dating of the letter (see below), so that we can simply refer to the commentaries for fuller discussion of the alternative views.[7]

THE OCCASION OF THE LETTER

The letter seems to have been written in immediate response to what Paul perceived as an urgent crisis among the Galatian churches (1.6–9). Since he had been with them, probably for the second time (4.13),[8] others had come among them urging them to be circumcised (5.2–12; 6.12–13). Paul calls them 'troublemakers' or 'agitators' (1.7; 5.10, 12), and it is probably a fair inference that they had criticized both Paul's claim to apostolic authority and his understanding of the gospel (1.1, 6–12), as perhaps also his consistency (5.11). Who they were, what they wanted for the Galatians and why, are central

---

[7] For the 'north Galatian hypothesis' see particularly J. Moffatt, *An Introduction to the Literature of the New Testament* (Edinburgh: T. & T. Clark, 1918) 3rd edn, pp. 90–101; W. G. Kümmel, *Introduction to the New Testament* (London: SCM, 1965) pp. 296–8. For the 'south Galatians hypothesis' see particularly E. de W. Burton *Galatians* (ICC; Edinburgh: T. & T. Clark, 1921) pp. xxvii, xxix, xliv; F. F. Bruce, 'Galatian Problems. 2. North or South Galatians?', *BJRL* 52 (1969–70) pp. 243–66; C. J. Hemer, *The Book of Acts in the Setting of Hellenistic History* (WUNT 49; Tübingen: Mohr, 1989), ch. 7; S. Mitchell, 'Galatian', *ABD* 2.871.

[8] *To proteron* probably means 'the first time', but could be translated simply as 'once' (BAGD, *proteros* 1).

questions for any study of the letter's theology, since the letter was evidently written directly to counter their teaching. These questions therefore need somewhat fuller attention than those touched on already.

The opponents

Who were the troublemakers whom Paul clearly perceived as opponents of the truth of the gospel (cf. 2.5, 14)? Some think they were gentile converts of Paul who had been impressed by the importance of circumcision in Jewish tradition, not least in the Abraham story of Gen. 17.9–14, and had become convinced that participation in the blessing promised to Abraham was impossible without it.[9] This view can certainly be defended on the basis of 6.13 (which can be translated 'those who are circumcised', but may very properly be rendered 'those who are being circumcised or are having themselves circumcised'). But the fact that Paul always refers to the troublemakers in the third person, while addressing his converts in the second person, strongly suggests that the two groups were distinct. Moreover, the emphasis throughout the letter indicates that the terms of the dispute were Jewish through and through, and probably so perceived through Jewish eyes. For example, Paul makes a point of asserting his Jewish identity at the beginning of the letter and of re-emphasizing the centrality of Israel at the end (1.13–14; 6.16). The parallels cited by him in chapter 2 were those of Jews insisting on traditional Jewish terms for acceptance of Gentiles. And circumcision was demanded of would-be proselytes precisely because it was so fundamental to Jewish identity – so fundamental that Paul can use the term to designate Jews as a whole as 'the circumcision' (not 'the circumcised' – 2.7, 9).[10]

Most commentators therefore conclude that the agitators were Jews. But even if they were not Gentiles seeking to

[9] See particularly J. Munck, *Paul and the Salvation of Mankind* (London: SCM, 1959), pp. 130–4; L. Gaston, *Paul and the Torah* (Vancouver: University of British Columbia Press, 1987), e.g. pp. 29–30, 81–2.
[10] See further below, ch. 2.

proselytize, Paul's converts were. That is to say, the Jewish 'troublemakers' seem to have been enjoying considerable success in persuading Paul's Gentile converts on the need to be circumcised.[11] This points at once to the heart of the letter and one of its principal theological issues. It can be expressed in several ways: how do Gentile and Jew relate to each other within the purposes of God? How should Gentiles relate to the God of Israel? How can Gentiles participate in the blessings God promised through Abraham? Who belongs to Israel now that Messiah Jesus has come and on what terms? Is circumcision after all to continue to be the key identity factor which marks out the assembly of God's people? No study of the theology of Galatians can avoid giving this issue central place.

It is even clearer that the 'troublemakers' were, like Paul, Christian Jews, that is, believers in Jesus as Messiah and followers of his 'way' (Acts 24.14, 22). This is obvious inference from the fact that Paul acknowledges, however grudgingly, that they claimed to preach the 'gospel of Christ' (1.6–9), since the word 'gospel' was already a distinctively Christian term.[12] They likewise seem to have agreed with Paul on the importance of faith in Christ (cf. 2.16) and of the cross of Christ (6.12).[13] What was at issue was the corollary to these fundamentals (3.1–5, 15–18; 4.9–10).[14] Here again is matter of prime significance for understanding the theology of the letter. For it expresses a dispute between Christians, a dispute about the fundamental question of the gospel itself. It reminds us that the formative theology of Christianity was forged not simply and not primarily under attack from without, but as a wrestling of Christian with Christian (including Paul with Peter! – 2.11–18) to understand what it was that constituted the essential character of Christianity. Here again we are reminded of

[11] The repeated use of the present tense in the letter (1.6; 4.9–10, 21; 5.2–4; 6.12) indicates an on-going crisis, with increasing numbers succumbing to the new teaching.

[12] See particularly P. Stuhlmacher, *Das paulinische Evangelium* (Göttingen: Vandenhoeck, 1968); also 'The Pauline Gospel', *The Gospel and the Gospels*, ed. P. Stuhlmacher (Grand Rapids: Eerdmans, 1991), pp. 149–72.

[13] See further below chs. 2 and 3.

[14] See further below ch. 4.

the living quality of the letter's theology and of the model for
theology which it provides.

If then the opponents were Christian Jews who had come to
the Galatian churches from outside, who were they and how
should we refer to them? 'Troublemakers' is, of course, Paul's
own way of referring to them and hardly provides an unbiased
description, rather the irascible response of one who felt his
authority under threat. Traditionally they have been called
'judaizers', meaning those who attempt to bring others within
Judaism. This is unfortunate since the word is drawn directly
from the Greek, *ioudaizein*, which means 'to live like a Jew,
according to Jewish customs',[15] *not* to impose Judaism on *others*.
Furthermore, the latter, inaccurate meaning reinforces a view
of Judaism as strongly evangelistic at this time, which although
also widely held, is again almost certainly false, at least as an
appropriate generalization. Gentile God-fearers and especially
proselytes were, of course, welcome within Judaism, but as a
rule the impetus came from without rather than from within.[16]
The first full-scale missionary movement (properly so-called)
by Jews to Gentiles that we know of was the missionary outreach of the Jews who believed in Jesus Messiah and followed
his way.

In fact, the 'troublemakers' were themselves probably part
of that missionary outreach, though, as appears obvious, a
different strand from that of Paul. This is implicit, as we shall
see shortly, in Paul's defence of the legitimacy of his apostleship
and gospel (1.1, 11–12). For at this very early stage in Christianity 'apostle' still retained its primary meaning of 'one sent

---

[15] Esther 7.17 LXX – 'many of the Gentiles were circumcised and judaized for fear of
the Jews'; Theodotus in Eusebius, *Praeparatio Evangelica* 9.22.5 – Jacob would not
give Dinah to the son of Hamor 'until all the inhabitants of Shechem were
circumcised and judaized'; Josephus, *War* 2.454 – Metilius (commander of the
Roman garrison in Jerusalem) 'saved his life by entreaties and promises to judaize
and even to be circumcised'; Josephus, *Ant.* 20.38–46 – Izates, king of Adiabene,
having been converted by a Jewish merchant, without circumcision being required,
was thereafter persuaded that circumcision was essential.

[16] See particularly S. McKnight, *A Light Among the Gentiles. Jewish Missionary Activity in
the Second Temple Period* (Minneapolis: Fortress Press, 1991); M. Goodman, 'Jewish
Proselytizing in the First Century', *The Jews among Pagans and Christians in the Roman
Empire*, ed. J. Lieu et al. (London: Routledge, 1992), pp. 53–78.

out', that is, in this context, 'missionary'. Moreover, the still clearer implication of 1.8–9 is that they had come to Galatia 'preaching the gospel'. In consequence they are most simply referred to as 'the other missionaries'.

Can we be more precise? J. L. Martyn argues that the 'troublemakers' were 'a law-observant mission to Gentiles' independent of Paul's, and prefers to call them simply 'the Teachers'.[17] This is less likely, since Judaism's unconcern for evangelistic outreach to Gentiles seems to have been shared by the first, Jerusalem-centred Christians. According to Acts the first outreach to non-Jews was by Hellenists (Acts 11.20),[18] who were persecuted for their *lack* of law-observance (Acts 6.13; cf. Gal. 1.13–14 with Phil. 3.5–6). Even Peter, to whom Acts attributes the first, surprising and unwillingly recognized breakthrough to Gentiles (Acts 10.1–11.18), was authorized only for missionary work among 'the circumcision' (Gal. 2.7, 9). Moreover, the prominence Paul gives to clarifying his relations with Jerusalem and the Christian leadership there (Gal. 1.15–2.10) strongly implies that authorization from Jerusalem was a major plank in the other missionaries' platform, both in criticism of Paul's gospel (hence Paul's vigorous defence) and in their claims for the validity of their own version (which Paul attacks in turn – 1.6–9). It is not simply that Paul was responding to the other missionaries (the point which Martyn emphasizes), true though that is. It would be more accurate to say that Paul was responding to *their* response to *his* earlier preaching in Galatia.

All this suggests that what Paul was confronting in Galatia was a determined attempt to undo (as Paul would see it) or to complete (as the other missionaries would see it) Paul's work in Galatia. That is, we should probably envisage a group of Christian Jews, who understood it to be their missionary task to ensure that Gentile converts to 'the way' were properly

[17] J. L. Martyn, 'A Law-Observant Mission to Gentiles: The Background of Galatians', *SJT* 38 (1985) pp. 307–24.

[18] It is perhaps worth noting here that the descriptions of earliest Christianity as 'the way' all come in references to the Hellenists persecuted by Paul (Acts 9.2; 22.4) or to Paul's own practice as a Christian (24.14; cf. 24.22) or in relation to Paul's own missionary work (19.9, 23; cf. 18.25–6).

converted, that is, had realized the full implications of this Jewish faith, and who claimed the authorization of the Jerusalem church's leadership for their mission. In their view the Gentile Galatian converts could not claim participation in the full heritage of Israel's blessing simply as God-fearers; they must become full proselytes.[19] All this is thoroughly bound up with the theology of the letter itself and will require fuller discussion as we proceed. But for the moment the above outline must suffice.[20]

The date

The issue of the date has usually been made to depend on the debate between the north Galatian and south Galatian hypotheses. Those who argue for the south Galatian hypothesis mostly do so as a way of integrating the account of Gal. 1 and 2 with the accounts in Acts. The two visits of Jerusalem of which Paul speaks in Gal. 1.18–20 and 2.1–10 are correlated with the visits of Acts 9.26–30 and 11.29–30. The result is that Galatians can be dated prior to the 'Jerusalem council' of Acts 15, that is, to about AD 48 or 49. On the other hand, those who find the north Galatian hypothesis more persuasive, and who see in 4.13 a reference to two visits to (north) Galatia, have to date the letter after that second visit (presumably referred to in Acts 18.23), which means a date somewhere in the mid-50s.[21]

The disagreement does not amount to much. To be able to date an ancient document to within six years of its composition would satisfy most historians. And since in either case the letter would come from a mature man (at least in his forties), already well experienced in his life's vocation, and presumably, therefore, with an already well-developed theology, it hardly seems worthwhile to pursue the issue further. Moreover its resolution

---

[19] The episode of the two-stage conversion of Izates, king of Adiabene, around about this time is probably the nearest parallel (Josephus, *Ant.* 20.38–46), and Matt. 23.15 should probably be understood in the same terms.

[20] The suggestion that Paul was also battling on a 'second front' (against Gnostics or pneumatics/spiritists) has gained little favour; see, however, R. Jewett, 'The Agitators and the Galatian Congregation', *NTS* 17 (1970–1) pp. 198–211.

[21] See again those cited above in n. 7.

is so bound up with questions about the historical value of Acts and about Acts' relationship to Galatians, problems which seem to be fairly intractable and to which I can offer no fresh or simple solution, that it would detract too much from the purpose of this volume even to review the various arguments on either side.

However, the issue has some importance in regard to the letter's theology, precisely because it raises the question as to whether its theological argument is already mature and long-established, or is being freshly minted within the letter. In Galatians is Paul *citing* theology, drawn from a larger and already well-formed system, or is he *doing* theology, creating, perhaps even *de novo*, what later generations have recognized to be primary statements of theological principle? The later the date, the less likely that Galatians is an original or primitive expression of the Pauline gospel. Moreover, the relation of Galatians to the other main Pauline letters comes into question: was it written after the Corinthian correspondence and within a year or two of Romans (as the north Galatian hypothesis is usually thought to imply)? In which case it is a fiery restatement of what was already well established within a wider Pauline mission to the Gentiles, and it would be fully valid to interpret Galatians by reference to the only slightly later Romans.

In fact there are various clues within the theology of Galatians itself which have not been given enough weight in such discussion, and it is worthwhile drawing out their implications for the date and circumstances of the letter precisely because of their theological significance.[22]

(1) One is the probable outcome of the confrontation between Paul and Peter at Antioch (2.11–14) and its sequel. For it is very unlikely that Paul's rebuke was accepted by Peter, otherwise Paul would surely have trumpeted the fact (as he did in 2.6–9), so important would it have been for his Galatian audiences to know this.[23] And despite his being

---

[22] For discussion of other theological indices of date see particularly R. Longenecker, *Galatians* (WBC 41; Dallas: Word, 1990) pp. lxxxiii–lxxxviii.

[23] There is a growing consensus within current scholarship on this point.

thus effectively isolated among his fellow Jewish believers, all of whom, including Barnabas, sided with Peter (2.13), Paul evidently had no intention of changing his tune (2.15–21). Consequently we have to envisage a breach opening up between Paul on the one hand and Jerusalem on the other, since it was evidently at the instigation of the group 'from James' (by then undisputed leader in Jerusalem) that Peter had so acted (2.12). This also implies a fairly radical disagreement opening up on how the agreement so recently won at Jerusalem (2.6–10) should be interpreted.

From Jerusalem's perspective it would follow that the interpretation of the agreement thus confirmed at Antioch should extend to the daughter churches established by the mission from Antioch.[24] But these were precisely the churches established by Paul, while he was a missionary commissioned from Antioch (Acts 13–14). Some kind of follow-up mission, able to claim authorization from Jerusalem, therefore, was only to be expected. This obviously fits well with the south Galatian hypothesis and suggests a date not long after the Antioch incident.

(2) This fits in turn with two other pieces of evidence from the letter itself. First, the cry of anguish in 1.6 at the speed of the Galatians' defection ('so quickly'). This need not mean 'so quickly after Paul's departure from among them', but that is certainly one of the two main options for understanding what Paul says, and its probability is strengthened by the degree of 'fit' with the other implications being drawn out here. That is to say, the text invites a reconstructed scenario in which Jewish missionaries quickly sought to capitalize on the outcome at Antioch and to reinforce a more traditional understanding of Gentile con-

---

[24] We should simply note that the so-called 'apostolic decree' of Acts 15.20–9 was sent explicitly to 'Gentiles in Antioch and Syria and Cilicia' (15.23), that is, to the region administered from Antioch, and so to churches which would naturally fall within Antioch's 'sphere of influence'. But the manifold problems relating to the historicity and terms of the 'apostolic decree' make it difficult to draw any further or firmer deductions from it relating to the Galatian question.

version to a Jewish 'way' of life in churches established by Paul.[25]

Second, the manner in which Paul's rebuke of Peter at Antioch merges into his plea to the Galatians in 2.15–21 strongly suggests both that Paul saw the parallel between what happened in Antioch and what was happening in Galatia, and that he was in effect restating his argument to Peter for the benefit of the Galatians.[26] An argument which he lost at Antioch he hoped to re-express more forcibly and with greater effect. This suggests that the Antioch incident was still vividly alive in Paul's memory, and indeed that his failure there was something still deeply and sharply felt by Paul. Again this does not demonstrate that Galatians was written within months rather than years of the Antioch incident, but it certainly strengthens that impression.

(3) To mention but one other point, which emerges from a comparison between Galatians and the other undisputed Pauline letters. Two themes receive particular emphasis in Galatians – the fact of Paul's apostleship (1.1, 11–12, 15–16; 2.7–9) and the central importance of 'justification' (2.16–3.24). In contrast, in Thessalonians Paul does not introduce himself as an 'apostle', a feature otherwise absent only in the friendly letters of Philippians and

---

[25] The fact that the demand upon the Galatians was for circumcision, a step beyond what seems to have been in view at Antioch, and in violation of the Jerusalem agreement (2.3–6), may be explained in one or more of several ways: the other missionaries were building on the Antioch triumph and pressing beyond to a more consistent Jewish position; the conversion of the complete pagans of Galatia was seen as a step more threatening to Jewish self-identity than winning the allegiance of proselytes and God-fearers in Antioch; Paul's defeat at Antioch was thought to have largely nullified his earlier victory at Jerusalem; or the other missionaries of Galatia in fact belonged to the 'more conservative wing' of the church in Jerusalem (the 'false brothers' of 2.4). See further my *Galatians* (London: A. & C. Black, 1993), Introduction §6.

[26] 'It cannot be accidental that at the end of the *narratio* in Gal. 2.14, when Paul formulates the dilemma which Cephas is in, this dilemma is identical with the issue that Galatians themselves have to decide: "Why do you compel the Gentiles to judaize?"' (Betz, *Galatians* 62). A similar inference can be drawn from 2.4 ('in order that the truth of the gospel might remain for *you*') – that is, that Paul saw the issue posed earlier on at Jerusalem as likewise a close parallel to the issue confronting the Galatians.

Philemon; and the theme of 'justification' is noticeable by
its absence in Thessalonians, whereas it is common to all
Paul's other main letters. The point is that the Thessalonian correspondence is usually reckoned to be the earliest
preserved from Paul's pen. So it marks a time before, for
whatever reason, Paul had developed the practice of intro-
ducing himself as apostle or of emphasizing 'justification'.
Galatians, however, seems to mark Paul's awakening to
the need to stress both themes as of fundamental importance for his mission. This strongly suggests that Galatians
was written after Thessalonians, and that it was the Galatian crisis which established both themes firmly as features
of Paul's epistolary style and teaching. Here too other
explanations are possible, but here again, taken with the
other considerations, the probability can be reckoned as
stronger than most other hypotheses, that Galatians was
written between the Thessalonian and Corinthian correspondence.

In short, a very plausible hypothesis is that Paul wrote
Galatians from Corinth to the churches of south Galatia in the
early 50s, or, to be more precise, during the period from late
50 through the first half of 51; and that he wrote it to meet the
threat posed to his gospel to the Gentiles by Jewish Christian
missionaries from Antioch or Jerusalem, who had come to
Galatia in an attempt to improve or correct Paul's gospel.
Here again theological themes and issues are thoroughly
involved in what might at first seem to be merely technical
issues of dating, and most of what has been outlined above
depends on the fuller exposition and discussion which must
follow. But any exposition will involve some dialogue between
text and context, and this initial attempt to set Galatians
within its originating context must suffice for present purposes, at least as an opening exchange in the dialogue which
enables us in turn to engage in more circumspect and
thorough theological analysis.

It follows, of course, if the above outline and dating is
anywhere near correct, that Galatians is indeed Paul's first
recorded attempt to wrestle with major themes and funda-

mental principles of the Christian faith. Consequently, its already high theological interest becomes all the more fascinating, given also its vibrant and polemical character. Here indeed is theology in the making and worth wrestling with, if determined to win its blessing, till break of day.

CHAPTER 2

The make or break issues

It is important to remind ourselves that Galatians comes down to us as a letter and not as a theological tract or treatise. For it is the letter form which makes the whole document so personal and which gives its appeal such an emotive quality. Paul is addressing those he had come to know during his own visits to Galatia. In other words, the rhetoric of the document is not directed at an impersonal audience but to individuals he remembered and no doubt could have named. Moreover the relationship was one of mutual benefit. They had given him a warm and supportive welcome when he first arrived, apparently in some physical discomfort or worse (4.13–15). And they in turn had received the blessing of Paul's message, having been converted through his own ministry. The letter, then, was a means of renewing old relationships, a substitute for a personal presence which distance made impossible (4.20).[1] It was a personal message delivered by letter because Paul perceived the need as urgent and because, presumably, his own circumstances made a visit in person impracticable.

The main bulk of the theology lies, of course, in the body of the letter. Comparison with other letters of the time provides a strong indication of just how freely Paul adapted the letter form to suit his own purposes, particularly in the solid theological character of the body of his letters. Nevertheless it is wise to begin by taking account of the framework of the letter, that is, the introduction and conclusion. For it is there that epistolary conventions were most likely to be followed and

[1] See e.g. J. L. White, *Light from Ancient Letters* (Philadelphia: Fortress Press, 1986) pp. 218–20.

indeed were largely followed by Paul, the letter writer. And for the same reason, it is there that departures from normal convention will be most noticeable. Moreover, it is in the introduction, where the initial attempt was being made to reestablish the old personal rapport, that indicators were likely to be flagged up of what Paul considered to be of central importance in constituting or reconstituting his relationship with the Galatians. Just as it is the personal character of the final parting which was likely to ensure that central concerns of the letter were recalled in summary.

Whether these considerations are more widely true of Paul's letters, they are certainly relevant for a study of Galatians. We begin, therefore, by looking at the issues which come to the surface in the introduction and conclusion of the letter.

INTRODUCTION

According to epistolary convention – that is, according to the normal writing habits of the reasonably well educated – a typical letter would include the following elements in its introduction:

A (author) to B (recipients);
greeting (*chairein*);
thanksgiving and prayer for recipients.[2]
It is instructive, therefore, to note where Paul conforms to this convention and how he departs from it – 1.1-9.

Standard form	*Paul's standard form*	*The unique features in Gal.*
Paul,	apostle –	not from human beings nor through a human being, but through Jesus Christ and God the Father, who raised him from the dead –
	and all the brothers with me,	

---

[2] See e.g. W. G. Doty, *Letters in Primitive Christianity* (Philadelphia: Fortress Press, 1973) pp. 27–33.

to the churches
of Galatia.   Grace to you and peace
                     from God our Father
                     and the Lord Jesus
                     Christ,   who gave himself for our sins,
                                                       in order that he might rescue
                                                       us from the present evil age, in
                                                       accordance with the will of our
                                                       God and Father; to whom be
                                                       glory for ever and ever, amen.
I am astonished   that you are so quickly
                                                       turning away from the one
                                                       who called in the grace (of
                                                       Christ) to another gospel,
                                                       which is not an other, except
                                                       that there are some who are
                                                       disturbing you and wanting to
                                                       turn the gospel of the Christ
                                                       into something else. But even
                                                       if we or an angel from heaven
                                                       preach to you a gospel con-
                                                       trary to what we preached to
                                                       you let him be accursed! As we
                                                       said before, I now say also
                                                       again: if anyone proclaims to
                                                       you something contrary to
                                                       what you received, let him be
                                                       accursed!

To start with, Paul naturally identifies both himself as
sender and those to whom he writes: 'Paul ... to the churches
of Galatia'. He also immediately includes his own characteristic Christian adaptation of the usual greeting: 'Grace (*charis*)
to you and peace from God our Father and the Lord Jesus
Christ'.[3] But apart from that the conformity to convention
ceases. It is this departure from normal form, and even from his
own usual literary practice, which gives the first clue to the
personal and pressing concerns which motivated his writing of
the letter.

First, he adds the descriptive title – 'Paul, an apostle'. As
already noted, that seems to have become his practice thereafter. What is unparalleled even within his own correspondence, however, is the addition of a highly defensive descrip-

[3] Exactly as in Rom. 1.7; 1 Cor. 1.3; 2 Cor. 1.2; Phil. 1.2; 2 Thess. 1.2; Philem. 3.

tion of the origin of his apostleship – 'not from human beings nor through a human being, but through Jesus Christ and God the Father ... ' (1.1). Moreover, the abruptness with which he adds this parenthesis indicates a considerable degree of agitation and sense of urgency. Clearly then the status of Paul's apostleship in the eyes of his Galatian audiences was a matter of primary concern to which we must give more attention.

Second, he adds what look like two already well-established confessional or worship formulae: ' ... God the Father, who raised him from the dead' (1.1); and ' ... our Lord Jesus Christ, who gave himself for our sins to set us free from the present evil age, according to the will of our God and Father' (1.4). These presumably indicate basic Christian convictions common to Paul and his readers. They were evidently non-controversial between them (they are cited rather than argued), and as such no doubt formed an integral part of the personal bond which bound Paul and the recipients of his letter together – echoes, perhaps, of preaching themes and formulae used by Paul when he had first preached the gospel to them, and not contested by the other missionaries. We will have to return to them in chapter 3.

Third, and just as striking as the first, is Paul's failure to offer thanksgiving and prayer on behalf of his readers.[4] Those of his readers accustomed to the courtesies of friendly correspondence were bound to be taken aback by such impoliteness, and would probably have been stunned by the abruptness and violence of the assault which Paul launches instead – 'I am astonished that you are so quickly turning away from the one who called in the grace (of Christ) to another gospel, which is not an other ... ' Here evidently for Paul was a second point of great sensitivity, which will also repay closer attention.

---

[4] S. K. Stowers, *Letter Writing in Greco-Roman Antiquity* (Philadelphia: Westminster, 1986) pp. 21–2; Longenecker, *Galatians* p. 13. Contrast Rom. 1.8–10; 1 Cor. 1.4–9; Phil. 1.3–11; Col. 1.3–12; 1 Thess. 1.2–10; 2 Thess. 1.3–4; Philem. 4–7. The use of *thaumazo* ('I am astonished') is well attested as a rebuke formula in Greek papyrus letters (see G. W. Hansen, *Abraham in Galatians. Epistolary and Rhetorical Contexts* (JSNTS 29; Sheffield Academic, 1989) pp. 33–44), but not in Paul.

Paul's apostleship

The obvious inference to draw from the first parenthesis (1.1) is that Paul believed his claim to or understanding of apostleship to be under challenge. It is not clear how the challenge had been made: the other missionaries (we can assume it was they) may have attacked Paul's claim directly, or indirectly – that is, simply by asserting their own authorization as (by implication) superior to Paul's. Nor is it quite clear what the criticism of Paul's apostleship amounted to. Judging by Paul's vehement response (*'not* from human beings, *nor* through a human being'), the other missionaries maintained either that Paul's apostleship had come through human channels (through Peter, cf. Gal. 1.18; or Ananias, cf. Acts 22.12–16; or Antioch, cf. Acts 13.1–3),[5] or possibly even that it lacked any human recognition at all (at least in its more controversial features). Either way, the authority of the Jerusalem Christian leadership itself would outweigh Paul's, and Paul might well be expected to acknowledge this. Whatever the finer details, it is sufficient for our understanding of the letter's theology that Paul felt it necessary to defend himself, with his very first breath and before he had even greeted his Galatian audiences.[6] Clearly the matter was one of greatest sensitivity for Paul – presumably because it was the basis of his whole relationship with the Galatians.

What was evidently at stake in Paul's mind was the meaning of apostleship and its legitimation. Part of the problem was the fact that the concept itself was developing in significance. As already noted, the word (apostle) means simply 'one sent, commissioned as an emissary'. Elsewhere Paul uses it of delegates from one of his churches (2 Cor. 8.23; Phil. 2.25). But it had already gained a more important sense, of one commis-

---

[5] It is certainly significant that the only time Luke describes Paul as an 'apostle' is during his 'first missionary journey', on which he embarked precisely as a missionary (= apostle) of Antioch, and indeed during his mission among the towns of southern Galatia (Acts 14.4, 14). This is the first of a number of points at which Luke's account in Acts may reflect something of the views of Paul's *opponents* (see also below p. 136 n. 5).

[6] We shall need to remind ourselves on several occasions that Paul wrote his letter to be read out to and *heard* (not read) by the Galatian congregations.

sioned by Jesus himself. This sense probably derived first from the tradition of the resurrection appearance of the risen Christ which Paul himself inherited (1 Cor. 15.7). Certainly it was this sense which Paul was anxious to claim for himself (1 Cor. 15.8–9).

The problems emerged as a result of two tendencies pulling against each other. On the one hand, Paul seems to have pushed the meaning of apostle of Jesus Christ hard in the direction of apostle = one sent out, missionary, that is 'church-founder' (1 Cor. 9.1–2); and in his case, he insisted, that meant missionary to the Gentiles (Gal. 1.15–16; 2.8). On the other hand, the word was closely bound up with the importance of the twelve, as those historically closest to Jesus, commissioned during Jesus' ministry,[7] the first group of witnesses of the resurrection (1 Cor. 15.5), and therefore holding a normative role as his first apostles. This is reflected in the way in which Acts uses 'apostles' almost exclusively for and as synonymous with the twelve (Acts 1.2, 26; 2.37, 42–3; etc). In contrast, it may be significant here that Paul leaves the status of James ambiguous (Gal. 1.19),[8] perhaps unwilling to recognize as an apostle one who seems to have remained throughout in Jerusalem.

This tension probably lies behind and helps to explain the double emphasis in Paul's treatment of the theme in Galatians.

His primary emphasis is clear. His authority as apostle was not dependent on any human source or medium; it came direct from the risen Christ himself (1.1). The importance of the point for Paul is further indicated by the way he heavily underlines it in what serves as the thematic statement for the rest of the first two chapters: 'For I want to make clear to you, brothers, that the gospel preached by me is not of human origin. For it was not from a human being that I received it, neither was I taught it, but through a revelation of Jesus Christ' (1.11–12). The

---

[7] Note that the use of *apostolos* in reference to the twelve in Matthew and Mark is confined to their role as those sent out by Jesus on mission (Matt. 10.2; Mark 3.14; 6.30).

[8] 1.19 can be taken to mean either 'the only other apostle I saw was James', or 'I saw no other apostle, the only person I saw was James'.

human authority he had in mind becomes clear in 1.16–21: it was Jerusalem, or, to be more precise, the leadership of the Jerusalem church. Thus Paul takes pains to emphasize that he did *not* hasten to Jerusalem immediately after the 'revelation of Jesus Christ' to him on the Damascus road in order to gain an authoritative interpretation of his vision,[9] but went away, instead, into Arabia (1.16–17). It was only three years later that he went up to Jerusalem, and then simply 'to get to know Peter'; he did not even *see* anyone else of significance except James (1.18–19); the testimony was so important to Paul that he vouches for its truth with an oath (1.20). Paul's point so far, then, is clear: his authorization as missionary was direct from God through Christ; it had already been clearly understood by him before he ever went up to Jerusalem; and his mere 'getting to know you' visit to Peter was not a significant or determining factor in his subsequent fourteen years of missionary work in Syria and Cilicia (1.21).

At the same time, the very force of Paul's denial amounts to an acknowledgment that if any human authority was of relevance on this issue it had to be Jerusalem. The tension between direct commissioning from God and human validation of that commissioning is therefore already apparent. The tension becomes even more evident as Paul proceeds. For in his second visit to Jerusalem, albeit some fourteen to seventeen years after his original commissioning,[10] Paul was anxious to gain the recognition of the Jerusalem leadership. Without it his mission would have been 'in vain' (2.2). They had authority to compel Titus to be circumcised, if they so chose (2.3 probably implies this), or to 'add something' to Paul (2.6). But in the event, Paul's arguments and the evident success of his mission to date seem to have won the day, and instead the pillar apostles

---

[9] The verb (*prosanethemen*) as used here evidently had a technical sense of consulting someone about the significance of some sign – a dream, or omen, or portent, or something of that order; for details see my 'The Relationship between Paul and Jerusalem according to Galatians 1 and 2', *NTS* 28 (1982) pp. 461–78, reprinted in *Jesus, Paul and the Law. Studies in Mark and Galatians* (London: SPCK/Louisville: Westminster, 1990) pp. 108–28, here 109–10.

[10] Most agree that the 14 years of 2.1 should be taken *in addition to* the 3 years of 1.18, but Paul could have meant 14 years *including* the earlier mentioned 3 years.

acknowledged his commissioning to the Gentiles and gave him the right hand of recognition and friendship, to that extent at least acknowledging his apostleship (2.7–9).[11]

Here then a classic theological issue is immediately posed: what is the primary force in the word 'apostle'? Is it divine commissioning or human authorization? Can one be sustained without the other? Is the central function of apostleship the founding of new churches (so that it could later be used appropriately of those who established new denominations), or continuity with and so recognition from the original twelve? Paul strikes a careful balance which may provide something of a model. Of course, it is no doubt the case that Paul was happy to acknowledge the authority of the Jerusalem leadership because in the event they had exercised that authority to affirm his own apostleship; whether he would have been so amenable otherwise remains an open question. Nevertheless, the balance he did achieve between independent commissioning and ecclesiastical validation provides a good illustration of the tension which must be maintained between what we might call the immediacy of charismatic inspiration and the regulating force of official recognition. This is a larger point to which we will have to return in chapter 6.

It would be a mistake, however, to interpret this issue as primarily one of Paul's personal status. For it is equally clear that Paul defended his apostolic authority primarily as a way of defending his understanding of the gospel.

Paul's gospel

Where Paul really felt under threat was not so much for himself as for the gospel which he preached. As the thematic statement of 1.11–12 indicates, his apostolic commission was to preach the gospel, the gospel neither handed down to him by tradition nor taught him by human teacher, but given him by the immediacy of divine revelation. It was this gospel whose reception by the Galatians had been the start and basis of Paul's

---

[11] It is not entirely clear whether the second half of 2.8 should read, 'me for apostleship to the Gentiles', or simply 'me to the Gentiles'.

continuing relationship with them. The thought of his Galatian converts turning away from this gospel to another and different gospel left him stunned; the troublemakers were trying to turn the gospel of Christ into something else; the very possibility drew from Paul one of his most forceful denunciations and a repeated curse (1.6–9). It was 'the truth of the gospel' which he was prepared to defend against all comers, whether 'false brothers' in Jerusalem or Peter in Antioch (2.5, 14).

What Paul meant by 'the truth of the gospel' is hinted at in his reference to it as 'the gospel of Christ' and as focusing on God's call 'in grace' (1.6–7). This characterization of the gospel in terms of grace is a central element in Paul's theology in Galatians (1.15; 2.9, 21; 5.4), and we will have to take up other aspects of it later. For the moment, however, it is the link which grace forms between Paul's apostleship and his gospel on which we need to concentrate. The point is made when Paul describes his commissioning: 'But when it pleased the one who set me apart from my mother's womb, and called me through his grace, to reveal his Son in me, in order that I might preach him among the Gentiles ... ' (1.15–16). As the Galatians had been 'called in grace' (1.6; cf. 5.8, 13), so had Paul. That is to say, Paul's own experience on the Damascus road had demonstrated to him the essential character of the gospel. Moreover, this experience was also and primarily a commissioning (apostle-making) experience. And, most significant of all, it was a commissioning to preach this same gospel (the gospel of Christ, focusing on Christ, preaching Christ) *among the Gentiles*. In other words, the gospel and its truth was, for Paul, inextricably bound up with preaching that gospel and its grace to the Gentiles. That this is the nub of what was at stake for Paul is confirmed by the emphasis Paul puts on the agreement which he managed to achieve in Jerusalem. It was because they recognized the gospel entrusted to Paul for the uncircumcised, and 'the grace given' to Paul as attested by his success in winning Gentile converts, that James, Cephas and John, the leading men in Jerusalem, had given him the right hand of fellowship and formally recognized that Paul and Barnabas had indeed received a divine commissioning to take the gospel as preached by Paul to the Gentiles (2.7–9). Hence also Paul's characterization of God's word to Abraham as gospel ('preached the gospel beforehand to Abraham') because it promised blessing to 'all the nations' (3.8).

The issue, then, was to do with Paul's understanding of the gospel in relation to the Gentiles: integral to the truth of the gospel for Paul was that it was a gospel of grace for the Gentiles. This presumably throws light on the puzzle still left in 1.6–7: whether what the other Christian Jewish missionaries preached to the Galatians was in fact also the gospel. Paul denies that it was so, but his use of the phrase 'another gospel' almost certainly implies that the other missionaries spoke of their message also as the 'gospel', that is (it could hardly be other) 'the gospel of Christ'.[12] Judging by the emphasis Paul places on the gospel as expression of grace, and in response to the preaching of the other missionaries, that must mean that the latter objected to the degree of freedom which Paul's interpretation allowed as an over-emphasis on grace (cf. 5.1). Paul's preaching gave too little or no place to the obligations which would usually be part of Gentile conversion to a Jewish movement, circumcision in particular.[13]

The theological issue at stake becomes more precise when we realize that in chapter 2 Paul again speaks of two gospels, defining them as 'the gospel of uncircumcision', with which he had been entrusted, and 'the gospel of circumcision' entrusted to Peter (2.7). In both cases (chapters 1 and 2), 'for the Gentiles' is at the heart of the one gospel, and 'of circumcision' is at the heart of the other. And yet Paul denounces the one circumcision gospel (1.6–9) while seeming content to recognize the other (2.7–9). What made the difference? The answer must be that in the first case (chapter 1, in Galatia) there was a lack of mutual recognition and acceptance: the other missionaries had criticized Paul's gospel as inadequate, and Paul denounced their gospel as no gospel. Whereas in the second case

---

[12] See above ch. 1 n. 12.
[13] See further ch. 5 below.

(chapter 2, in Jerusalem), each had recognized and accepted the other. To be more precise, they had recognized the validity of different forms of the gospel in different contexts (among Jews for Jews, and among Gentiles for Gentiles), and had agreed not to try to preach or enforce their understanding in the other's context.

Here then is a nice theological conundrum. When is the gospel not the gospel? The reality is that there were (and are) different interpretations of the one gospel of Christ, and Paul's hard won point in Jerusalem was that there could be different interpretations which are valid. It was the attempt to enforce a uniform *Jewish* understanding of the gospel in *Gentile* Galatia which roused Paul to furious indignation. Integral to the freedom of the gospel is freedom to express it differently, with different emphases in different contexts. There is, of course, much more to be said, for we have still to clarify what was involved in 'the gospel of Christ' and the grace of the gospel, but the make or break issue for Paul, as already indicated in the second paragraph of his letter, was clearly the character of that gospel as good news for the nations.

CONCLUSION

In accordance with epistolary conventions of the time,[14] Paul added a concluding paragraph in his own hand at the end of his dictation (6.11–18).[15] In this case in particular it was another and final opportunity to underscore his special concerns and the make or break nature of the issues confronting the Galatians. The absence of any personal greetings, in contrast to his normal practice, is presumably a further indication of Paul's agitation and depth of concern at the news from Galatia (cf. 6.17). What is striking, then, is that the conclusion consists in another impassioned plea regarding circumcision (6.12–16), involving a repeated antithesis between circumci-

[14] Betz, *Galatians* p. 312 n. 4.
[15] As also in 1 Cor. 16.21–4 and 2 Thess. 3.17; probably also Rom. 16.17–20 and Col. 4.18.

sion and the cross (6.12, 14–15; by implication also in 6.17). The point can be documented quite easily – 6.12–17.

Circumcision	*Cross*
It is those who want to make a fair showing in the flesh, they are trying to compel you to be circumcised,	but only to avoid being persecuted for the cross of Christ.
For even those who have themselves circumcised do not themselves keep the law, but want you to be circumcised in order that they might boast in your flesh.	But as for me, God forbid that I should boast except in the cross of our Lord Jesus Christ, through whom the world has been crucified to me and I to the world. For neither circumcision counts for anything, nor uncircumcision, but a new creation.
And as many as will follow this rule, peace be on them and mercy, as also on the Israel of God. From now on let no one cause me trouble.	For I bear the marks of Jesus on my body.

That Paul can pose the central concerns of the letter in terms of this repeated contrast between circumcision and the cross is bound to be significant for our understanding of Paul's theology in the letter and of the make or break issue as he saw it between his understanding of the gospel and that of the other missionaries.

Circumcision

There can be no dispute that the principal demand made by the other missionaries was for Paul's Galatian converts to be circumcised. The antithesis of the conclusion had already been spelt out in forceful terms in 5.2–6:

Look! I, Paul, say to you that if you are circumcised, Christ will benefit you not at all. I testify again to everyone who is being circumcised that he is obligated to do the whole law. You have been estranged from Christ, you who are seeking to be justified by the law; you have fallen away from grace ... For in Christ Jesus neither circumcision counts for anything, nor uncircumcision, but faith operating effectively through love.

Galatians itself does not explain why circumcision was such a crucial concern for the other missionaries. But the reason becomes immediately apparent when we set the text in its primary historical context. For, as already noted in chapter 1,[16] circumcision lay at the heart of Jewish identity, so much so that Jews as a people could be identified simply as 'the circumcision' (2.7, 9; similarly Rom. 3.30; 4.9; Col. 3.11). It was not that Jews were the only people to practise circumcision; it was rather that the importance they placed on the ritual marked them out from all other nations.[17] And again the reason is fairly obvious. Circumcision was important because, in accordance with the conditions laid down by God when it was first instituted (Gen. 17.9–14), circumcision was the mark of the covenant, the sign and guarantee of the special relationship between God and the descendants of Abraham, a seal on God's acceptance of Abraham and his seed (so also Rom. 4.11–12). Two centuries before Paul the importance of circumcision as Israel's essential identity marker had been massively reinforced by the Maccabean crisis: for the crisis had been occasioned by the attempt of Israel's Syrian overlords to destroy Israel's distinctiveness, precisely by forbidding circumcision (1 Macc. 1.48, 60–1); and the Maccabean defence of Judaism consequently had included among its first priorities the reassertion of circumcision as indispensable for all Jews (1 Macc. 2.46). Thus, for the great bulk of Jews, the link between 'Jew', 'Judaism' and circumcision was axiomatic; an uncircumcised Jew was virtually a contradiction in terms. And since circumcision was

---

[16] See above p. 8.

[17] The point was widely recognized: e.g. Josephus, *Ant.* 1.192 – God commanded Abraham to practise circumcision 'to the intent that his posterity should be kept from mixing with others'; and Tacitus, *Hist.* 5.5.2 – 'They adopted circumcision to distinguish themselves from other peoples by this difference.'

thus so inextricably bound up with the covenant promise to Abraham and his descendants, no one could surely think to have a share in that inheritance without being circumcised.

That this must have been the theological rationale of the other missionaries in Galatia is fairly obvious from this historical context. But it is also implied in the terms Paul uses in the Conclusion to the letter, and particularly in Paul's characterization of the motivation of the other missionaries: they 'want to make a fair showing in the flesh'; 'they want you to be circumcised in order that they might boast in your flesh' (6.12–13). Here Paul was presumably not thinking simply of the ceremony of circumcision as such (in the flesh), but also of the flesh as denoting ethnic descent and identity.[18] For the other missionaries, circumcised flesh would be a cause of boasting (6.13), because it marked out covenant identity and indicated participation in the heritage of Abraham even for the foreigner (Gen. 17.12–13). All this would probably have been so self-evident to the other missionaries that Paul's neglect of circumcision and objection to their requirement of it must have caused them some puzzlement. Quite why he should be so vehement on the point has yet to be fully clarified.

The cross

In contrast to the other missionaries' insistence on circumcision, Paul emphasized the cross. The verses already cited are full of indications and reminders to the Galatians of just how central the cross was to Paul's gospel. (1) It was Christian emphasis on the cross which was the occasion of persecution (6.12). Since readiness to circumcise Gentiles, such as the Galatians, is presented in this verse as a means of escaping such persecution, Paul must have had in mind *Jewish* persecution of the Christian Jewish outreach to the Gentiles – persecution such as he himself had engaged in before his own turn to Christ and the Gentiles (1.13). Where circumcision had been the cause of Gentile persecution of the Jews two centuries earlier,

---

[18] As in Rom. 4.1; 9.3; 11.14; 1 Cor. 10.18; also Gal. 4.23, 29.

the proclamation of Christ crucified now (3.1) was a scandal to
most Jews (5.11; cf. 1 Cor. 1.23) – an attitude shared at least to
some extent by the other missionaries themselves.

(2) Whereas the other missionaries wanted to boast in circumcised flesh, Paul's boast focused exclusively on the cross
(6.14); the cross was of such epochal significance that it relativized everything else, the distinction between circumcision
and uncircumcision not least (6.15; cf. 1.3). The same life and
death association between his personal experience and the
epochal significance of the cross had already been indicated by
Paul in 2.19–21.

(3) It is the mark of the cross branded in his body, the proof
of his commissioning by the crucified and risen Christ, which
enabled Paul to dismiss those troublemakers with their insistence on the lesser mark of circumcision (6.17).[19]

There is much in all this which again requires further attention, and we will need to enquire more closely, particularly
within the body of the letter, as to what fuller theology lies
behind these summary statements. Here it is sufficient to draw
attention to the fact that Paul could set circumcision and the
cross in such direct opposition to each other. Evidently a clash
of fundamental principles for Paul (and the other missionaries)
was involved, and the attempt to clarify what precisely these
make or break issues were, and what were their ramifications,
is bound to be fruitful for our understanding of the theology of
the letter.

One final hint should not be ignored at this point however.
For if the working hypothesis of this chapter is correct, then
fundamental issues are posed and summarized in the introduction and conclusion. It presumably follows that the make
or break issues in both cases are related to each other. That is to
say, Paul's apostleship and gospel will have centred not simply
on Christ, but on the cross of Christ in particular. And Paul's

[19] There is a strong consensus that by 'the marks of Jesus' themselves Paul means the
scars and physical effects of the various beatings and severe hardships (including
being stoned) which Paul had already experienced in the course of his missionary
work (2 Cor. 11.23–7). The thought therefore links up with his talk elsewhere of
sharing Christ's sufferings and death (Rom. 8.17; 2 Cor. 1.5; 4.8–10; Phil. 3.10; Col.
1.24); in Gal. see 2.19, 5.24 and 6.14, and below ch. 5.

understanding of the cross of Christ will have been at the heart of his understanding of his apostleship and gospel as to the Gentiles and for the Gentiles (so particularly 3.13–14). In the same way the issue between Paul and the other apostles was about the integrity and legitimacy of an apostleship authorized by a (Jewish) Messiah to take the gospel of a crucified (Jewish) Messiah to uncircumcised non-Jews.

CHAPTER 3

The fundamental agreements

A major problem in writing on the theology of a single document is whether the document is to be read as a statement of theology sufficiently complete in itself or as a witness to a fuller theology which is presumed to lie behind it. On the first alternative, commentators may be hopeful that their reconstructions of the document's theology will properly reflect the emphases of the document itself. But they will be bound to leave many questions unanswered, where features are unclear, including presumably, allusions or echoes which can be neither identified not illuminated from the text itself. On the second alternative, there is an equal danger that the real focus of interest will become the fuller theology lying behind the document and that the distinctive features of the document's own emphases will be lost sight of or too readily discounted.

In this case we can surely presume that a larger theology of Paul does indeed lie behind Galatians. The theology of Galatians is like a basin of water drawn from a larger cistern. It can be taken for granted, in other words, that in Galatians Paul neither wrote everything he could have written on any subject, nor attempted to write on every appropriate subject. And of course, behind Paul there is a larger theology again – that of the first Christians, in all its diversity. And behind them again the theologies of the wider Judaisms of the time, to go no further. It is clear, however, that for this volume the focus must be on Galatians itself, and not on any of these larger theologies lying behind it. At the same time, Galatians is so closely related to its specific context of controversy, and to Paul's earlier preaching (to the Galatians in particular – 1.6–9, 11; 2.2–5;

3.1; etc.), that without some awareness of these wider theologies it will be impossible to recognize allusions and echoes for what they are and their function within the letter, and to that extent we will be incapacitated in our attempt to sketch out the theology of the letter itself. Fortunately the access which we have to Paul's other letters and our contemporary knowledge of Second Temple Judaism put us in a strong position to recognize these allusions and echoes. And since we will limit our objectives to illuminating the echoes and allusions of the letter itself, our focus will remain on the theology of the letter as such.

So far as Galatians itself is concerned, then, we can identify a number of shared convictions – shared both between Paul and the other missionaries, and between Paul and the Galatians – the shared perspective and experiences which distinguish these convictions as Christian. Because they belong to Paul's assumptions, and assumptions which Paul shared with the recipients of the letter, we should not expect to find them developed in detail in the letter itself. Indeed in most cases it is sufficiently clear from Paul's reference that he was able to make such a brief reference because the point was a matter of agreement. In a strict sense, therefore, it might be argued that they do not belong to the developed theology of Galatians itself. But they are part of the submerged or hidden theology on whose resources Paul drew to build up his appeal to the Galatians, and they do provide the basis of that appeal. They therefore deserve attention as part of the foundations of the letter's theology. Moreover, it soon becomes evident that much of the controversy of which the letter was part was the result of different interpretations of these shared convictions. Some study of these fundamental agreements will therefore have a double benefit: it will remind us that behind the controversy there was a good deal of common ground; and that the controversial features of the letter's theology were Paul's attempt to interpret and work out these fundamental agreements.

THE SHARED CONVICTIONS

R. B. Hays has argued that 'the framework of Paul's thought is constituted neither by a system of doctrines nor by his personal religious experience but by a "sacred story", a narrative structure', that 'the story provides the foundational substructure upon which Paul's argumentation is constructed', and that without awareness of the story the theological discourse of Galatians is unintelligible 'because the discourse exists and has meaning only as an unfolding of the meaning of the story'.[1] This is a helpful way both of expressing the concerns outlined above and of characterizing the shared perspective common to Paul and to the other missionaries. Both were attempting, as we might say, to locate the Galatians or to help them find themselves by reference to a common story. Hays focuses his attention on the 'particular paradigmatic story about Jesus Christ',[2] but would agree that behind that story lies the larger story of Israel.

The story of Israel

The importance of the story of Israel is indicated at a number of points in Galatians. For a start, we cannot ignore the fact that in the first five verses of the letter Paul speaks repeatedly of God the Father (1.1 – 'God the Father'; 1.3 – 'God our Father'; 1.4 – 'the will of our God and Father'). The idea of God as Father was one deeply rooted in all the religious traditions of the Mediterranean world.[3] By implication it indicated the equivalent of a blood-tie between God and those begotten by him, with all the overtones of family solidarity and obligation to kin thus involved. But Paul would certainly be thinking in terms of the God and Father of Israel in particular (cf. e.g. Deut. 32.6; Isa. 63.16; Jer. 31.9). He did not need to say so

---

[1] R. B. Hays, *The Faith of Jesus. An Investigation of the Narrative Substructure of Galatians 3:1–4:11* (SBLDS 56; Chico, Scholars Press, 1983) pp. 5, 6, 21; cf. N. T. Wright, *The Climax of the Covenant. Christ and the Law in Pauline Theology* (Edinburgh: T. & T. Clark, 1991).

[2] Hays, *Faith*, p. 19.

[3] G. Schrenk, *pater*, *TDNT* 5.951–8.

explicitly, but none of his readers would have been in any doubt on the point. It was simply a matter of common assumption – that the God of whom Paul (and the other missionaries) spoke was, of course, the God of Israel. But even that would have been enough to evoke the whole story of Israel, as redeemed from Egypt and chosen by God, that he should be the God of Israel in particular (as classically in Deut. 32.6–9), and that they should live in accordance with his will as his people (the Torah).

In the light of this opening it is less surprising than it might have been that Paul should include in his conclusion a blessing 'upon the Israel of God' (Gal. 6.16). Who precisely Paul intended to embrace by that title is a question to which we must return. But it should be clear enough that by pronouncing the blessing Paul was at least evoking the whole history of Israel as the Israel of God, and that by implication this evocation would resonate with the Galatians (and the other missionaries) both meaningfully and attractively.

Other elements in the letter would also be dependent for their effect on some awareness of the story of Israel. For example, the technical sense of *euaggelizesthai*, 'to preach the gospel' (1.8), goes back behind the accounts of Jesus' preaching (Matt. 11.5; Luke 4.18; Acts 10.36) to the striking use of the term in Isaiah (Isa. 40.9; 52.7; 61.1) and would thus evoke the whole story of Israel's return from Exile.[4] Similarly with the language of *anathema* ('let him be accursed', 1.8–9). For though the term was known in Greek speech in the sense 'something dedicated',[5] it is the Old Testament sense of 'devoted to God in order to be destroyed' which dominates Pauline usage here (as elsewhere – Rom. 9.3; 1 Cor. 12.3; 16.22). To be meaningful to Paul's readers, they would have to be aware of such passages as Lev. 27.28–9 (relating to the cult), Deut. 7.26 (regarding Israel's treatment of the idols of other nations) and Josh. 6.17–18, 7.1, 11–13 (the story of Achan).

In 1.13–14 Paul recalls his 'way of life previously in

---

[4] Others within Second Temple Judaism found the language of Isaiah similarly evocative (*Pss. Sol.* 11.1; 11QMelch).

[5] BAGD, *anathema*.

Judaism', and his earlier zeal 'for the traditions of my fathers'. The reference indicates that he is speaking of a phase in his life now left behind, and we must reflect further on that below. But here we may note the implication obviously intended that Paul had a history (within Judaism) which he shared in some measure with the other missionaries. His reference to his persecution of 'the church of God' would have carried a similar resonance, for, almost certainly, by using the word, particularly in its singular form, Paul was intending to evoke the regular Old Testament usage where the term refers to 'the assembly of God', that is, the people of Israel gathered for consultation or worship.[6] The implication is, of course, that the church of Jesus Messiah which Paul had previously persecuted was in direct line of continuity with the assembly of the people of Israel.

The case is further strengthened when we recall the prominent place Paul gives to Jerusalem in Galatians: both in his own autobiographical narrative (1.17–18; 2.1–2 – if his gospel had not been affirmed in Jerusalem Paul would have been running 'in vain'); and in the allegory of 4.25–6. It is true, of course, that the latter reference contains a severe polemic against 'the present Jerusalem'. But here it is important to note that in evoking the whole theme of Jerusalem Paul was tapping into one of Israel's most potent symbols – Zion–Jerusalem.[7] As we shall see later, the idea of 'the Jerusalem above' is drawn directly from Jewish apocalyptic thought, even though controversially applied here. And the thought of Jerusalem as 'our mother' is likewise well rooted in Jewish thought.[8] What evidently was at stake in all this was the claim of continuity with Jerusalem (as historic symbol of Israel). The terms on which the claim was being made in respect of the Galatians were a bone of contention between Paul and the other missionaries. But common to them all was the recognition that the claim had to be made, that without the claim of

---

[6] See e.g. Deut. 23.1–2; Judg. 20.2; 1 Chron. 28.8; Neh. 13.1; Mic. 2.5.

[7] See e.g. Fohrer, *Sion, etc'*, *TDNT* 7.308–19.

[8] Cf. the LXX of Ps. 87.5 where 'Mother Zion' is addressed; also Isa. 50.1; 51.18; Jer. 50.12; Hos. 4.5; *4 Ezra* 10.7; *2 Bar.* 3.1

Jerusalem as 'our mother', with all that that included in terms of the appropriation of Israel's story, the claim that God was 'our Father' through the gospel could not stand.

It is hardly necessary to go on. But we should at least recall that the primary categories of Paul's debate in Galatians are drawn from and presuppose the story of Israel as fundamental to the self-understanding of the Gentile believers in Galatia. From the side of the other missionaries the emphasis on circumcision and law makes the point clearly, since it was precisely through circumcision and the law (from their perspective) that Gentiles could be incorporated into the history of Israel. That argument was disputed by Paul, and again it is one we must return to. But his own key category of 'righteousness' (Gal. 2.21; 3.6, 21; 5.5) was also wholly drawn from the distinctive terms of Israel's covenant faith. In Israel's self-understanding God was to be recognized as 'righteous' because he fulfilled the obligations which he had taken upon himself in entering into covenant with Israel, rescuing Israel and punishing its enemies,[9] restoring and sustaining Israel despite its sin.[10] Correspondingly, to be reckoned as 'righteous' by God was to be recognized as belonging to his people, members of that covenant, within the sphere of his righteousness/saving action.[11] for Paul no less than his opponents it was essential for the Gentile Galatians to be drawn into the sphere of God's saving action hitherto focused in Israel.

Finally, it should not go without mention that the whole argument of the central section of Galatians (chs. 3–4) revolves round the idea of sonship of Abraham. The reasoning is clear: sonship of Abraham was integral to Christian self-identity; one could not count oneself a Christian unless one also counted oneself a child of Abraham. We need not decide here whether this line of argument as a whole, or simply the appeal to the Genesis accounts of Abraham's fathering of Ishmael and Isaac, was first introduced to the Galatians by the other

---

[9] E.g. Exod. 9.27; 1 Sam. 12.7; Mic. 6.5.
[10] E.g. Pss. 31.1; 35.24; etc.; Isa. 46.13; 51.5.
[11] E.g. Pss. 5.12; 11.7; 34.15–22; Isa. 51.5, 6,8; 60.21; 63.1. See also ch. 4 below.

missionaries.[12] The point is that Paul does not refute such assumptions and claims. He too was wholly of the view that the Gentile Galatian believers should regard themselves as belonging to Abraham's seed and thus (and only thus) as sharers in Abraham's inheritance. However contrived his own defence of that view may initially seem,[13] it was clearly of first importance to Paul that he should be able to make that defence.

The theological significance of this is obvious. In contrast to some who want to argue that Judaism and Christianity have always been completely different religions or religious systems,[14] Paul thought it of vital importance to maintain the view that through the gospel Gentiles also were given to participate in the promise to Abraham and inheritance of Abraham (3.14-29; 4.23, 28, 30). Judaism and Christianity are of course separate religions now,[15] but these titles so used (Judaism, Christianity) refer to the distinctive forms which grew further apart following the parting of the ways early in the second century.[16] Galatians belongs to that earlier period when the common features of what were to become separate religions were much more obvious than their distinctive features. It is certainly unwise to speak of Christianity and Judaism as quite separate religions during the ministry of Paul;[17] and Paul himself never thought of his encounter on the

[12] So Martyn, 'Law-Observant Mission' in particular.

[13] But see below ch. 6.

[14] Somewhat surprisingly, the point has received particular emphasis from J. Neusner in recent years, e.g. *Jews and Christians. The Myth of a Common Tradition* (London: SCM/Philadelphia: TPI, 1991).

[15] We should, however, note the restoration of the continuum between Judaism and Christianity in the twentieth-century phenomenon of Messianic Jews in Israel and North America.

[16] See my *The Partings of the Ways between Christianity and Judaism* (London: SCM/Philadelphia: TPI, 1991); also J. D. G. Dunn, ed. *Jews and Christians. The Parting of the Ways AD 70 to 135* (Tübingen: Mohr, 1992).

[17] The point is easily confused because of what Paul himself says in 1.13-14, implying that 'in Judaism' marked a phase of his life now past. The confusion arises because Paul's 'Judaism' denotes a specific (Pharisaic) understanding of his Jewish heritage, whereas the same term used today of the first-century period (late Second Temple Judaism) covers the wider range of religious belief and practice maintained by Jews of the period (Judaisms – plural). Paul's usage in 1.13-14 should not be taken to mean, therefore, that Paul saw himself as having left behind the commonly recognized heritage of Jews as a whole, the religion of the Jews. Quite the contrary. See again my *Partings* chs. 2 and 8; also *Jews and Christians* pp. 177-211. F. Watson,

Damascus road as a conversion, let alone a conversion from Judaism, but rather as a commissioning within the prophetic continuum running from Isaiah and Jeremiah in particular.[18] Of course, the claim of continuity which Paul makes in Galatians and the particular arguments he used belong to the matters at serious issue between him and the other missionaries. But the significant point remains that Paul wanted to make that claim; he neither devalued nor discounted it; on the contrary, it forms a major part of his exposition of the gospel. For Paul the gospel of Christ would have been impossible to understand except as a means of fulfilling the promise to Abraham and as marking the line of continuity with God's saving purpose for Israel.

The story of the Christ

The second story which Paul assumes, alludes to and draws upon in Galatians is the story of Jesus. Superimposed upon the story of Israel was the story of Jesus as Israel's Messiah. It is true that 'Christ' had already become more or less equivalent to a proper name for Jesus by this time. But the facts remain that 'Christ' is the Greek translation of 'Messiah', that 'Messiah' was an important feature of Jewish expectation concerning the restoration of Israel in the age to come (e.g. *Pss. Sol.* 17.32; 1QS 9.11; Shemoneh 'Esreh 14), and that the complete identification of Jesus as the 'Christ' of Jewish hope lies beyond and must certainly have been the reason for it becoming a second identifying name for Jesus. Moreover, there may well be echoes of the titular force of Christ ($=$ the Messiah) at various points in the letter (1.6–7, 10; 2.20; 3.16, 24, 29; 5.24; 6.2, 12).[19] However such finer points of exegesis

---

Paul, Judaism and the Gentiles. A Sociological Approach (SNTSMS 56; Cambridge University Press, 1986) ch. 3, in arguing that Paul wanted the church to separate from the Jewish community, ignores the continuum maintained by the Jerusalem church and confuses what actually transpired with what Paul wanted to happen.

[18] See e.g. those cited in my *Jesus, Paul and the Law* p. 101 n. 1; A. Segal, *Paul the Convert. The Apostolate and Apostasy of Saul the Pharisee* (New Haven: Yale University Press, 1990) particularly ch. 4.

[19] The claim is made more strongly by Wright, *Covenant* ch. 3.

might be resolved, the claim that Jesus himself provides the link between Israel's earlier or pre-history is obviously at the heart of the letter (3.16, 29), and would no doubt have been shared with the other missionaries.[20]

Equally indicative of the importance of the story of Christ for Paul are the two formulaic passages he includes in the introduction, already referred to in chapter 2 (1.1, 4). The reason why Paul should cite them, and in a letter in which he cuts down the conventional pleasantries to a bare minimum, is presumably because they were part and evidence of his *bona fides*. They have the ring of a formula because they had already become well established within the Christian churches as summaries of the gospel which constituted them as church. As such they were part of the common foundation and fundamental agreements which were already giving the new term 'Christian' (Acts 11.26) its distinctive definition. So here it is most probable that Paul cites them, both within his opening sentence, as a way of reminding his readers of the gospel which united both Paul and his converts, and indeed any who claimed to be apostles/missionaries of Christ.

The first is added to the first reference to God the Father – 'who raised him (Jesus) from the dead' (1.1). Here at once the impression is given of one story superimposed on another. This is the Father God Paul is speaking of – not simply the God and Father of Israel, but more precisely the God who revealed and thus defined himself more clearly by raising Jesus from the dead. The one did not, of course, cancel out the other; rather, by implication, the second story (of Jesus) was to be understood as the outworking of the first (of Israel's God).

The language clearly echoes what was in fact probably the earliest credal-type affirmation of the first Christians.[21] As such it reflects the foundational character of the belief in Jesus' resurrection for the first Christians. Here it is the *only* qualifying or defining clause; there is, for example, no mention of Jesus' earlier life or of his death. That which really marked out

---

[20] See above p. 9.
[21] Cf. particularly Acts 3.15; 4.10; Rom. 8.11; 10.9; 1 Thess. 1.10; 1 Pet. 1.21. See further W. Kramer, *Christ, Lord, Son of God* (London: SCM, 1966), pp. 20–6.

God for Paul, in relation to his other and older beliefs regarding God, was the fact that he had raised Jesus from the dead. The authenticating force of the story of Jesus is focused in its climax in Jesus' resurrection. Of course Paul was looking to undergird the authority of the risen Christ (in appointing Paul as apostle!), and perhaps in distinction to those whose claims were rooted more or as much in their relationship with Jesus during his earthly mission (cf. 2.6 and Acts 1.21–2) or in their relation to these first (Jerusalem-centred) apostles. Nevertheless the hope for the effectiveness of his claim rested firmly on the fact that this was the most fundamental belief shared by all believers, the very core of their common confession and baptism (Rom. 10.9). The fact that Paul makes no further mention of Christ's resurrection in this, his most polemical letter, is itself proof enough that it was part of the foundational creed which united himself and his readers.

The second formula is added to the second reference to God and Christ, this time as descriptive of Jesus Christ – 'who gave himself for our sins' (1.4). This too is a recurring thought within the Pauline corpus, whether as a voluntary act of self-sacrifice as here and in 2.20,[22] or as an act of God (Rom. 4.25; 8.32). The variety of formulation indicates that the substance of what was being claimed was more important than any particular form of words. By adding 'for our sins' (as in Rom. 4.25), Paul indicates clearly enough that he was thinking in sacrificial terms.[23] He cites a similar formula in 1 Cor. 15.3, which he must have learned at or soon after his conversion; the early influence of Isa. 53 is hard to dispute behind the formula Paul uses in Rom. 4.25, as also the influence of Jewish thought about the sacrifice of Isaac in Rom. 8.32; and the plural 'sins' (rather than the more characteristically Pauline singular) also points behind Paul to an earlier Christian Jewish formulation.[24]

This echo of a formula which Paul himself learned at such an early stage of his own discipleship, and as a means of

---

[22] Cf. Eph. 5.2, 25; 1 Tim. 2.6; Tit. 2.14.
[23] So explicitly Eph. 5.2; cf. Rom. 3.25; 1 Tim. 2.6.
[24] See further my *Partings*, p. 70.

reaffirming the faith he shared with his readers, is obviously deliberate. That is all the more remarkable since it comes in a context in which Paul is insisting with great vehemence on the independence of his apostleship (1.1) and on the directness with which his gospel came to him from the risen Christ (1.11–12). It can only mean that Paul did not see the two themes as contradictory. Paul had been instructed in this basic feature of the story of Jesus when he himself first believed. But it was not this feature which was in dispute between him and his Galatian readers (or the other missionaries behind them). It was rather Paul's interpretation of this common credal faith – Paul's conviction, in particular, of what this dying of Jesus meant for Gentiles as well as Jews.[25] This was why, as already noted, the cross was such a make or break issue for Paul (2.19–3.1; 3.13–14; 4.5; 5.11; 6.12, 14). And this too will have been why Paul was so anxious to remind his readers as early as possible that the centrality of the cross was common ground between them – 'who gave himself for *our* sins'. Whatever the differences which were to be highlighted in what follows, and precisely because of those differences, Paul begins by stressing their agreement on this fundamental summary of the gospel.

That Paul should thus recall both the resurrection of Jesus and his sacrificial death within the opening sentence of the letter is a reminder of how fundamental was the story of Jesus for earliest Christian self-understanding and of how that story could be focused in these two climactic events of that story. But the underlying story of Jesus continually breaks the surface of the letter, and repeatedly strengthens the impression that it has been superimposed on the story of Israel to bring that story to climax and focus. Here again it is important to realise that the basic claim would be common ground among all parties to the crisis in Galatia. Paul draws more controversial deductions from these shared convictions, but the basic convictions were shared.

---

[25] This helps clarify the tension between 1.11–12 and 1 Cor. 15.3: Paul had indeed received the common core of the gospel when he first joined the Christians; it was his *interpretation* of it as freely applicable to the Gentiles which he attributed to the direct revelation of Christ.

Thus in 1.13–16 it was the story of Jesus in 'the revelation of God's Son' to Paul which transformed Paul's previous understanding of the story of Israel 'in Judaism', the controversy entering with Paul's understanding of the 'revelation' as a commissioning to 'preach God's Son among the Gentiles'. Similarly, as we shall see in 2.14–17, the inference can justifiably be drawn that the story of Jesus eating with sinners has been superimposed on the story of Israel as kept separate from sinners; so that for Peter to refuse table-fellowship with Gentile believers was tantamount, in Paul's eyes, to condemning Jesus' own ministry among sinners. Most striking of all, the Christ is the seed of Abraham (3.16), the end and goal of the story of the law (3.22–6); and the sending forth of God's Son is the climax of God's purpose for those under the law (4.4),[26] aimed to reproduce the story of the Son's relationship to God in those who believe in him (4.5–7).[27] Moreover, in 5.21 there seems to be an echo of Jesus' kingdom preaching.[28] And in 5.14 there is probably an echo of Jesus' teaching on love of neighbour, so that we should probably understand the subsequent reference to 'the law of Christ' (6.2) as a summary of the interpretation of the law lived out by Jesus in terms of the love command,[29] that is, the life and teaching of Jesus once again superimposed on the more traditional understanding of a people under the law.

Not least it must be of significance that the summary references to the cross already noted repeatedly serve the same function. The story of Jesus focused in the cross is superimposed upon the story of Israel focused in the law, but in such a way in Paul's exposition that the common ground becomes ground for a radical reappraisal of the law in its continuing role. The cross

[26] Most see here a reference to Jesus being sent from heaven; but the same language is used of prophetic commissioning (e.g. Jer. 7.25; Ezek. 2.3; Acts 22.21), and by Jesus himself (Mark 12.6 the closest parallel); see further by *Christology in the Making* (London: SCM, 1989) 2nd edn, pp. 38–44; cf. J. M. Scott, *Adoption as Sons of God. An Exegetical Investigation into the Background of* Huiothesia *in the Pauline Corpus* (WUNT 2.48; Tübingen: Mohr, 1992), pp. 165–71.

[27] Cf. particularly Hays, *Faith*, ch. 5; see also p. 119 n. 33 below.

[28] See below n. 41.

[29] See below ch. 5. Some, including Betz, *Galatians*, pp. 300–1 and Martyn, 'Law-Observant Mission', p. 315, think that Paul took the phrase over from his opponents.

in some measure at least renders the law inoperative (2.19–21). Hearing with faith the story of Christ portrayed as crucified leaves no scope for works of the law (3.1–2). The cross removes the curse of the law and opens the blessing of Abraham to the Gentiles (3.13–14). The summary review of the story of Jesus in 4.4–5 focusing in its soteriological function – 'born of woman, born under the law, in order that he might redeem . . .', that is, by his death (1.4; 3.13) – marks the end of the law's protective role (4.1–3). The story of the cross is a stumbling block for those who continue to read the story of Israel as epitomized in circumcision (5.11). It is the cross which should be the focus of boasting, not any distinctiveness of race or circumcision (6.11–14).

In short, the story of Jesus is clearly a fundamental presupposition for Paul's theology in Galatians, particularly in its focus on Jesus's death and resurrection. And not just for Paul, but also for both his Galatian converts and the other missionaries. All parties shared these basic convictions and understood them within the context of the more ancient story of Israel. Where the disputes began was in the way Paul now heard the two stories, and particularly in relation to each other. To these issues we must return, but there is one further element of the common convictions at which we need to look more closely before we go further, not least because it helps clarify the potential tension between the two stories.

The apocalyptic transition

By using the world 'apocalyptic' I mean to embrace both aspects which have traditionally been indicated by it – the idea of a 'revelation' (*apokalypsis*) from heaven concerning the divine mysteries behind the reality of the world, and particularly the unveiling of God's final (eschatological) purpose for humanity.[30] It was this revelatory, climactic significance of Christ which caused the first Christians to add the story of Jesus to that of Israel in the first place. This was the shared

[30] See particularly C. Rowland, *The Open Heaven. A Study of Apocalyptic in Judaism and Early Christianity* (London: SPCK, 1982).

conviction which united them as the Jewish group now being distinguished as 'Christians'.[31] In that sense all the parties to the Galatian dispute had superimposed the story of Jesus on the story of Israel. What gave Paul's understanding its particular twist was the way the 'revelation of Jesus Christ' impacted on him. The story of Jesus was not just the fulfilment of the story of Israel, but indicated that the purpose of God for Israel and the world had shifted into a different plane. Once again, in other words, it is a case of common convictions interpreted by Paul in what proved a controversial way.

The common ground is again indicated in the opening formulaic quotations. The familiarity of the first, 'who raised him from the dead' (1.1), can easily obscure its apocalyptic character. For 'resurrection from the dead' as a category stems directly from an apocalyptic outlook.[32] To be noted particularly is the disjunction implied between the present age/ history, which ends in death, and the belief in a new age and recreated life the other side of death, over which death has no more hold (Rom. 6.9–10). The point here then is the conviction that Jesus had already experienced this 'resurrection'; in his case it had not awaited the end of world history (as preliminary to final judgment). In Jesus' resurrection a new age had dawned.

The point is reinforced by the second formulaic phrasing – 'who gave himself for our sins to rescue us out of the present evil age, according to the will of God' (1.4). Here again 'the present evil age' presupposes the Jewish apocalyptic schema which saw

---

[31] Hence the famous quotation of E. Käsemann, 'Apocalyptic was the mother of all Christian theology', in his 'The Beginnings of Christian Theology', *New Testament Questions of Today* (London: SCM, 1969) ch. 4 here p. 102; see also my *Unity and Diversity in the New Testament* (London: SCM/Philadelphia: TPI, 1990) 2nd edn, ch. 13. L. J. Martyn, 'Apocalyptic Antinomies in Paul's Letter to the Galatians', *NTS* 31 (1985) pp. 410–24, and J. C. Beker, *Paul the Apostle* (Philadelphia: Fortress Press, 1980), ch. 8, both emphasize the importance of apocalyptic in Paul's theology. But Martyn thinks that the emphasis is Paul's, over against that of the other missionaries; whereas my argument here is that an apocalyptic perspective belonged to the shared convictions which united the first Christians. And Beker surprisingly maintains that 'the Christocentric focus of Galatians (has pushed) Paul's theocentric apocalyptic theme to the periphery' (p. 58).

[32] As expressed most typically in such passages as Dan. 12.2; *1 Enoch* 51.1–2; *Apoc. Mos.* 13.3; 28.4; 41.3; 43.2; *2 Bar* 50.2; not to mention Matt. 27.52–3.

both world history as divided into two ages, the present age and the age to come, and the present age as one dominated by evil, in contrast to the glories of the future age. The contrast comes to explicit expression only in the two classic examples of Jewish apocalyptic, *4 Ezra* and *2 Baruch*,[33] which were written after AD 70. But it was a natural outworking of such seminal passages as the visions given in Dan. 2 and 7, and was implicit in Qumran's talk of 'the time of wickedness' (CD 6.10, 14; 12.23; 15.7; 1QpHab. 5.7), as in various sayings recalled in the Jesus tradition (Matt. 12.32; Mark 10.30; Luke 20.34–5). Paul certainly had no doubts that the present age was marked by corruptibility, superficiality, folly and blindness,[34] or that humankind as heirs of Adam were caught under the reign of sin and death (Rom. 5.12–21; 1 Cor. 15.20–2). The point is that the death of Christ had somehow rescued the communal confessing or worshipping 'us' from this evil age. On this eschatological significance of the death and resurrection of Jesus all these first Christians were agreed. The question outstanding was how this eschatological significance of the story of Jesus related to the ongoing significance of the story of Israel – a major bone of contention, as we shall see.

The same apocalyptic perspective informs the letter throughout. On the one hand, Paul emphasizes that the coming of faith in Christ was a matter of divine revelation (3.23) and that his own understanding of the gospel was given him 'through a revelation of Jesus Christ' (1.12) and by God 'revealing his Son in me' (1.15) – in each case the language using the technical apocalyptic terminology, and having the sense both of heavenly unveiling and climactic turning point in the divine purpose. On the other, Paul is equally anxious to warn against false or deceptive messengers from heaven (1.8;[35] cf. 3.19 and 4.14), and against other spiritual powers which

---

[33] *4 Ezra* 6.9; 7.12–13, 50, 113; 8.1; *2 Bar.* 14.13; 15.8; 44.11–15; also *2 Enoch* 66.6.

[34] 1 Cor. 1.20; 2.6, 8; 2 Cor. 4.4; Eph. 5.16 is a close parallel.

[35] The angelic interpreter was a standard element in Jewish apocalypses – the heavenly messenger (the word can be translated both 'angel' and 'messenger') who gave the stamp of heavenly authority to the message he delivered (Ezek. 8; Dan. 10; *1 Enoch* 1; *2 Enoch* 1; *Apoc. Zeph.* 2; *4 Ezra* 2.44ff.; 4).

restrain humanity within the enslaved state of the old age (3.21–4; 4.3–4, 8–10).

Here again we can see how what would be common ground between Paul and the other missionaries could quickly give way to matters of dispute. Both would no doubt have agreed that God's sending of his Son marked 'the fulness of time' (4.4). The imagery is of a container being steadily filled (the passage of time) until it is full.[36] The implication is of a set purpose of God having been brought to fruition over a period and its eschatological climax enacted at the time appointed by him (cf. 4.2; Eph. 1.10; Mark 1.15; Heb. 1.2).[37] This conviction that the eschatological climax had *already* arrived was the shared conviction of all first Christians, so far as we can tell. It was what that meant for the law which caused the dispute.

J. L. Martyn has drawn particular attention to the way in which Paul's thought is structured in Galatians in a series of what he calls 'apocalyptic antinomies'.[38] This is most immediately obvious, once again, in the conclusion penned with his own hand (6.13–14), where Paul sets in sharp antithesis 'the world', which has been crucified to him and he to the world, and the 'new creation'. As regularly in Paul, 'the world' denotes the totality of the whole creation (human as well as non-human) in its distance from God, and as yet unredeemed state.[39] Here it is equivalent to 'the present evil age' (1.4; so also e.g. 1 Cor. 2.6–8 and 2 Cor. 4.4). As the antithetical opposite, the 'new creation' must therefore mean the age to come (cf. Rom. 8.19–22 and 2 Cor. 5.17), that is, presumably the context of human existence made new, recreated, to serve as a fitting habitat for God's children (Rom. 8.21). The astounding claim of the first Christians is that the transition had already been made in effect for those 'in Christ'. Here indeed, as Martyn points out, are 'two different worlds'[40] – the

---

36 For the range of meaning see BAGD, *pleroma*.
37 G. Delling, *pleroma*, *TDNT* 6.305; F. Mussner, *Galaterbrief* (HTKNT 9; Freiburg: Herder, 1977) 3rd edn, pp. 268–9.
38 Martyn, 'Apocalyptic Antinomies'.
39 E.g. Rom. 3.6, 19; 5.12–13; 1 Cor. 1.20–1; 2.12; 6.2; 7.31–34; 2 Cor 5.19; 7.10. See further H. Sasse, *kosmos*, *TDNT* 3.892–3.
40 Martyn, 'Apocalyptic Antinomies', p. 412.

old world replaced through the apocalyptic shift of the cross by the new creation.

Martyn is also justified in seeing the effect of this apocalyptic shift in the rest of the letter. It is implicit in the powerful enunciation of 3.28 – 'there is neither Jew nor Greek, there is neither slave nor free, there is no male and female, for all you are one in Christ Jesus'. For these were precisely the distinctions and stratifications which characterized the old age – a world characterized and determined in its working by deep and often sharp divisions between races, between social classes and between sexes. The apocalyptic shift brought about through the cross was a shift from that kind of world to a new creation characterized and determined by Christ and his self-giving on the cross. The language implies a radically reshaped social world as viewed from a Christian perspective, equivalent to the 'kingdom-perspective' which informed Jesus' ministry, and with the same eschatological perspective and motivation (cf. 5.21).[41] Given that Paul may be quoting here another piece of common confessional faith (cf. 1 Cor. 12.13 and Col. 3.11) it was presumably more widely shared, but once again the particular twist he gave to 'neither Jew nor Greek' would no doubt be part of the controversy in which he was embroiled in Galatia.

Equally emphatic is the antinomy of flesh and Spirit in 5.16–24 – flesh and Spirit each set against the other. Here again the perspective is apocalyptic and the antithesis is between two worlds, present evil age and new creation – a cosmic force rooted in the human condition and a cosmic force from heaven implacably hostile to each other. Those who yield to the one will not inherit the kingdom of God (5.21). This single evocation of a principal theme of Jesus's teaching (the kingdom of God) would be enough to ensure that the passage as a whole would have a sympathetic hearing in the churches of Galatia, since much of it was commonplace anyway. But once again Paul does not hesitate to remind his Galatian readers of

---

[41] The imagery of 'inheriting the kingdom of God' in 5.21 is formulaic (1 Cor. 6.9–10; 15.50; Eph. 5.5; James 2.5) and probably reflects the influence of the Jesus tradition (Mark 10.17 par.; Matt. 25.34; Luke 10.25).

the points of key significance for him: to belong to Christ was to re-enact the self-giving and mortification of the cross (5.24); and, more controversially, law belongs together with flesh on the side of the antithesis opposite to the Spirit (5.18).

Most striking of all is the elaborate sequence of antinomies Paul develops in his allegory of Hagar and Ishmael (4.21–31). We will return to it in more detail later. All that we need note here is the way, once again, Paul works in the apocalyptic perspective in his talk of 'the Jerusalem above'. Here Paul clearly had in mind the strand of Jewish apocalyptic thought which presumed that there was a heavenly Jerusalem, that is, an ideal form of Jerusalem in the purpose of God, waiting, as it were, in heaven to be revealed at the end time, when God's purpose would be completely fulfilled. This was obviously based on Exod. 25.9, 40 (cf. Wisd. Sol. 9.8), where Moses was told to construct the tabernacle in accordance with the pattern shown him on the mountain. Hence the apocalyptic hope of the imminent revealing of this heavenly Jerusalem (*2 Bar.* 4.2–6; *4 Ezra* 7.26; 13.36).[42] The same apocalyptic schema is presupposed elsewhere in the New Testament, particularly in Hebrews (Heb. 8–10 – 8.5 explicitly citing Exod. 25.40) and Revelation (Rev. 3.12; 21.2–3, 10–11, 22–7). The corollary of such a schema, particularly in apocalyptic thought, is that the present equivalent is an inadequate copy, provisional and insubstantial, awaiting eschatological transfiguration into or replacement by the intended ideal.

All this we might expect to be sufficiently obvious, and indeed acceptable, to the other missionaries (and to the Galatian Gentiles familiar with such Jewish thought); the idea of the heavenly Jerusalem was common ground. But once again it was the twist which Paul applied which would have caused the offence – the present Jerusalem not simply as a shadow of the heavenly, but as in slavery and even to be rejected (Gal. 4.24, 30). To understand how Paul could have moved so far from such initial, shared convictions is the great challenge to

---

[42] Enoch speaks of his going 'up to the highest heaven, into the highest Jerusalem' (*2 Enoch* 55.2 – longer recension); see further e.g. E. Lohse, '*Sion etc.*', *TDNT* 7.325–7.

those who seek to grasp the substance of Paul's theology in Galatians.

THE SHARED EXPERIENCE

So far we have looked only at the convictions shared between Paul and those for whom he wrote – the common ground which he did not need to traverse afresh in this letter, but on which he nevertheless hoped to build a structure of persuasive arguments. But it is important to realize that what provided the close bond between Paul and the Galatian congregations was not simply a set of convincing arguments or beliefs. There was also the bond of shared experience. The importance of an intensely personal engagement with the gospel is an integral feature of Paul's autobiographical narrative in chapters 1 and 2: for Paul himself it had been a deeply inward encounter (1.16 – God was 'pleased to reveal his Son in me'); the individual equivalent of the apocalyptic transition was a death and life transformation of the centre of personal consciousness (2.19–20; 6.14). Hence the immediate appeal to his audiences' own experience of receiving the gospel at the beginning of the letter's central argument (3.1–5; 'Have you experienced so much in vain?', 3.4);[43] and the climax in the appeal to the shared experience of sonship, where the unconscious transition back and forth from second person to first person plural indicates again the assumption of shared experience (4.5–7). All this had evidently given a rich spiritual dimension to the warm personal bond already established by the welcome Paul received among the Galatians (4.14–15), and helps explain the deeply personal way Paul felt slighted by their subsequent behaviour (1.6–9; 3.1).

In other words, the preaching and receiving of the gospel in Galatia had not been simply a cerebral transaction, but a personal encounter of deep and transforming power. No doubt it was because the message reached into innermost depths, provided answers to real personal questions or touched the

---

[43] Although *epathete* used absolutely would naturally have a bad sense ('suffer'), a more neutral sense was quite possible and is most appropriate here ('experience').

springs of deep feeling and motivation, and drew into a community of those similarly moved, that it spoke with such effect
to mind as well. How else, we might ask, could the account of
an obscure prophetic figure in Judea and the astonishing
claims regarding his death and resurrection have met with
much credence in the cities of far off Galatia? The precise
workings of the dynamic interaction between psychological,
social and cognitive factors is one we can hardly hope to
describe in any detail in a case so remote in time and culture. It
is important, however, to note that such an interaction was
fundamental in the conversion of the Galatians, and that Paul
found it essential to appeal to this shared experience as much as
he appealed to their shared convictions.

The two principal features of shared experience to which
Paul appeals are summed up in the words faith and Spirit.

Faith in Christ

Traditionally in Christianity 'faith' has denoted both the body
of Christian teaching ('the faith', *fides quae*) and the act of
believing (*fides qua*) Christianity's claims. The former is derived
from the latter. Fundamental for Christianity has been the
recognition of the need for an inner attitude of acceptance and
trust on the part of the individual. 'Conversion' is the event
when that faith is first expressed, when the non-believer
becomes a believer. It was such faith as shared by many others
which made it possible for the same word to be used for the
common object of belief ('the faith').

Of considerably interest in Galatians is the fact that we see
already, in so early a document of Christianity, this very
process under way. 'Faith' was the common denominator
which bonded the first Christians together. Paul could speak
simply of 'those of faith' (3.7, 9), 'those who believe' (3.22),
'the members of the household of faith' (6.10), presumably
because faith, the act and attitude of believing, was the
common characteristic, indeed the defining characteristic of
those so referred to. It must be because this faith was so
distinctive a feature of the new movement that already it could

be used in a way approaching the objective usage so common later on: Paul 'now preaches the faith which once he tried to destroy' (1.23); he can speak of 'the coming of this faith' (3.23, 25), referring back to the faith and believing just spoken of in 3.22. 'You are all sons of God through this faith' (3.26). To be sure, Paul can express both the shared experience of faith and the shared conviction regarding Christ's death in intensely personal terms (2.20 – 'the life I now live in the flesh I live by faith which is in the Son of God, who loved me and gave himself for me'), but this will hardly be because he thought to claim a unique experience of faith, rather because he saw his own experience as characteristic of believers as a whole.

At all events, it is this shared faith to which Paul appeals at the beginning of his main argument: 'was it by works of the law that you received the Spirit or by hearing with faith? ... I ask you again, he who supplies the Spirit to you ... is it by works of the law or by hearing with faith?' (3.2, 5). The phrase translated 'hearing with faith' itself contains something of the ambiguity just referred to, and could be translated as 'by the message (that which is heard) of faith'.[44] But in context the thought is more on how the Galatians received the message than on the message itself, and in the closely parallel passage in Rom. 10.14–17 the thought is the same. So almost certainly Paul intended to recall his readers to the way the Galatians had responded to his preaching – that is, as an act of accepting the message of Christ crucified (3.1) and of opening themselves in trust to the one so proclaimed. It should be noted that this recall to the initial experience of faith stands at the head of the following exposition and argument of which faith is the central motif. Paul must therefore have been supremely confident that he was representing the matter correctly and that his Galatian audiences would have a warm personal memory of their own experience of thus coming to faith and of thus becoming part of 'those of faith' (3.7, 9).

It is equally important for the theology of Galatians to recognize that the fundamental character of faith was some-

---

[44] Most exploit the phrase's ambiguity in different ways: e.g. NEB/REB – 'by believing the gospel message' (similarly, NIV, NJB and NRSV).

thing accepted also by Christian Jews generally, including the other missionaries. This was already implicit in the first reference to 'faith' as a quotation of what the churches of Judea said about Paul: the characterization of the new movement as 'the faith' began with Christian Jews (1.23). And it will hardly be accidental that the second reference to faith is Paul's recollection of his appeal to Peter as an appeal to the shared conviction and experience of faith (2.16). The latter verse is much controverted, but there can be little dispute that Paul describes justification by faith as common ground shared by Christian Jews: 'We Jews by nature ... knowing that a person is not justified by works of law but only through faith in Jesus Christ' (2.15–16).[45] Again it is significant that Paul recalls this exchange just at the point where the recollection of the incident at Antioch is beginning to give way to the appeal directly to the Galatians with the other missionaries in the background, where, as already noted, 'faith' is the dominant theme.

All this needs to be stressed when talking of the common assumptions shared between Paul and those for whom he was writing. For, of course, the significance of this shared assumption was the primary bone of contention between Paul and his Galatian opponents. The way Paul can pose 'faith' and 'law' in sharp antithesis (3.12), and can define the apocalyptic shift dividing the story of Jesus from the story of Israel precisely as 'the coming of faith' (as though faith had been absent before) (3.23, 25), is sufficient indication that Paul saw much more at stake than we have so far uncovered. Likewise the way Paul focuses a sequence of key purpose clauses in the goal of faith (2.16; 3.14, 22, 24) indicates that faith plays a more crucial role for Paul than his opponents were likely to recognize. To all this we must return in the next chapter. For the moment, however, it again needs to be stressed that the experience of faith, of accepting and acting upon the shared convictions outlined above, was part of the common bond linking all the first Christians together and already beginning to define them in their social distinctiveness as 'Christians'.

---

[45] See also above p. 39.

So far we have spoken for the most part simply of 'faith'. This is justified by the fact that Paul too speaks so often simply of 'faith' as the defining characteristic of the new movement (characteristically in chapter 3). However, it can be taken for granted that the faith which marked out the first Christians (Jews and Gentiles) was faith in reference to Messiah Jesus. This is implicit in the fact that the shared convictions focused so much in the story of the Christ (see above): their conversion had been a divine calling in the grace of Christ (1.6); the gospel had come to Paul 'through a revelation of Jesus Christ' and had Christ as its central content (1.12, 16); the Galatians' faith had been in direct response to the portrayal of Christ crucified (3.1–2); and so on. Not least of importance is the equally clear implication that the faith involved was not simply an intellectual acceptance of certain claims regarding Jesus (his death and resurrection), but an act of commitment on the basis of that belief – a believing 'into Christ Jesus' (2.16), a being baptized into Christ and a putting on Christ (3.27) – expressed no doubt in the confession of Jesus as (my) Lord and in baptism in his name (cf. Rom. 10.9; 1 Cor. 1.12–13).

The phrase which encapsulates this feature is 'faith in Christ Jesus' (2.16; 3.22; also 2.20). That it is a crucial phrase is indicated by its position in the first two texts just mentioned: 2.16 – 'knowing that no human being is justified by works of the law but only through faith in Jesus Christ, so we have believed in Christ Jesus, in order that we might be justified by faith in Christ and not by works of the law'; 3.22 – '... in order that the promise might be given from faith in Jesus Christ to those who believe'. Whatever else Paul is doing in these passages, he is making an argumentative point. He evidently wanted to give 'faith in Christ' a more decisive role than his opponents. In other words, this phrase itself embodies the tension which runs through the letter – the tension between convictions and experiences shared by Paul, the Galatians and the other missionaries, and the particular emphasis Paul wanted to give it. All were agreed on the fact that the story of the Christ must be superimposed upon and thus somehow modify the story of Israel. All were agreed that faith was a common denominator, that the faith of paradigmatic Abraham must be more closely defined in terms of faith in the Christ. It was the extent to which faith in Christ refocused faith as experienced by Abraham which caused the controversy. Here again, then, are issues to which we must return, but once again in the light of the clarification already achieved regarding shared convictions and experiences.

The exposition so far should help to clarify and resolve an old dispute regarding this phrase which has been recently revitalized: whether the phrase translated 'faith in Christ' should not be better translated 'faith of Christ', 'Christ's faith'.[46] The strength of the suggestion is that the phrase can then be taken as an evocation of the underlying story of the Christ – 'the faith of Christ' understood as a shorthand reference particularly to Christ's faithfulness to death on the cross.[47] It would also parallel the emphasis in chapter 3 on the faith/faithfulness of Abraham (3.6–9). The point then would be that it is the faith(fulness) of Christ which brought about the apocalyptic transition to the new age and which thus marked out the new age as the coming of faith.

The difficulties with this view, however, are severe. The grammatical form of the phrase tells us nothing decisive either way.[48] But several other considerations carry more weight. For one thing, so much of the thrust of the letter is on the Galatians' response to the messages preached to them: 'faith' in its regular sense of 'belief or trust in' fits into that very naturally; whereas signals to the reader that the phrase should be taken in the sense 'the faithfulness of Christ' are notable by their absence. For another, 'faith in Christ' has verbal parallels (2.16 – 'we have believed in Christ Jesus'; 3.22), whereas Paul never speaks of Christ 'believing'. For another, the parallel in

---

[46] See especially Hays, *Faith* ch. 4; M. D. Hooker, *'Pistis Christou'*, *NTS* 35 (1989) pp. 321–42, reprinted in her *From Adam to Christ. Essays on Paul* (Cambridge University Press, 1990), pp. 165–86. I have argued against both in my 'Once More *Pistis Christou'*, *SBL Seminar Papers 1991* (Atlanta: Scholars Press, 1991), pp. 730–44.

[47] So particularly Hays, *Faith*.

[48] Cf. Mark 11.22 – 'faith of = in God'; Acts 3.16 – 'faith of = in his name'; Col. 2.12 – 'faith of = in the working of God'; 1 Thess. 2.13 – 'faith of = in the truth'; Phil. 3.8 – 'knowledge of God'.

chapter 3 is between Abraham and Christians, not between Abraham and Christ: 'those of faith' are evidently those who believe as 'Abraham believed' (3.6–7); and with the rest of the 'faith' references in chapter 3 functioning in effect as exposition of the thematic statement of 3.6–7 it would be surprising if Paul expected his readers to take 3.22 in a different way.[49]

Finally we might note the difficulty of meshing the 'faith of Christ' interpretation into the theological argument of the letter as it has begun to be unfolded above. Were the phrase solely an allusion to the story of Christ and particularly his death, it would refer only to the convictions shared by Paul and those for whom he was writing. Whereas, as already noted, the emphasis on the 'in order that' in both 2.16 and 3.22 indicates that the phrase encapsulated the point at issue between Paul and the other missionaries. Whatever the precise point of issue we would naturally expect that the main argument of the letter would focus on that and spend time expounding it. But we find no attempt made or need felt by Paul to expound the theme of Christ's faithfulness. Whereas the emphasis on faith, believing as Abraham believed, is clear and unequivocal. Presumably it was because the point was so important that Paul repeats it with such emphasis in the two most disputed verses: 2.16 – '... but only through faith in Jesus Christ, so we have believed in Christ Jesus, in order that we might be justified by faith in Christ ...'; 3.22 – '... in order that the promise might be given from faith in Jesus Christ to those who believe'. Clearly Paul wanted to give an emphasis to the shared experience of faith which his opponents did not share. Why that should be so still needs further clarification. For the moment, however, we can simply repeat that 'faith in Christ' was part of the common ground between Paul and those for whom he was writing, and that his appeal to the Galatians begins from the evocation of the experience of faith which they shared and which had brought the Galatians into the new movement focused on Jesus the Christ.

---

[49] Hays, *Faith* pp. 150–7 takes 3.11 as a reference to Christ, but has been followed by very few, even of those who agree with his 'faith of Christ' reading.

The Spirit of Christ

The other shared experience was clearly the Spirit. It is important to realize just how much weight was placed by the first Christians on the visible impact and transforming effect of the gospel on those who responded in faith. It was the tangible and evidently indisputable success of Paul's preaching among the Gentiles which had convinced the pillar apostles in Jerusalem to recognize that God worked with Paul for the Gentiles as much as with Peter for the circumcision (2.7–9). Without the manifest effects of this grace (understood as a transforming power, not just as an attitude of mind) Paul's plea for a circumcisionless gospel to the Gentiles would almost certainly have failed. The impact was the same as that related by Luke in Acts 10.44–8 and 11.15–18: where God had so signally manifested his acceptance of the Gentiles in question, how could anyone, devout Jew not least, refuse to accept them?

With similar logic Paul right at the beginning of his main argument refers his Galatian audiences back to the event and experience which marked the beginning of their lives as Christians. The starting point of their Christian experience was their reception of the Spirit. That was the primary datum for any assessment of their standing before God. That was the decisive transition point from which all else followed. That must therefore provide the basis of his theological argument as it had when he made the same plea in Jerusalem (2.7–9).[50]

I want to learn from you only one thing: was it by works of the law that you received the Spirit, or by hearing with faith? Are you so foolish: having begun with the Spirit are you now made complete with the flesh? Have you experienced so much in vain? If it is indeed in vain. So I ask again, he who supplies the Spirit to you and works miracles among you, is it by works of the law or by hearing with faith? (3.2–5).

To be noted is the way Paul could take for granted that his readers would know what he was talking about. Clearly he was recalling events of which he had been part and witness. Clearly

---

[50] Spirit and grace are two sides of the same coin in Paul's theology; see my *Jesus and the Spirit* (London: SCM, 1975), pp. 201–9, and below p. 105.

he felt able to assume that his Galatian audiences would both remember the events well and agree with his description of them. And equally clearly the appeal is to experience. Paul does not deduce the presence of the Spirit among the Galatians from other theological principles (you believed the message, you were baptized, therefore you can deduce from that that you also received the Spirit). Rather the appeal to their reception of the Spirit is direct. It was *that* which they could be expected to remember most vividly. Faith might be confused with a merely rational acceptance of logical arguments. But the reception of the Spirit was a powerful experience which evidently left a profound impression on all who participated. It marked a decisive new beginning (3.3); it involved experiences which they should not want to go back on (3.4); it was attended by miracles (3.5). How could they fail to remember such experiences and realize their significance?[51]

The significance was, as in the case of Cornelius, already referred to. To have received the Spirit was to receive it from God – 'he who supplies the Spirit' (3.5). It therefore signified God's acceptance – and evidently so clearly and indisputably that neither they themselves nor the other missionaries could or evidently were willing to question it.

The importance of this beginning experience of the Spirit is indicated by the way in which Paul recalls it regularly throughout the rest of the letter (3.14, 27; 4.5–7, 29; 5.1, 5, 7–8, 16–18, 21–2, 25; 6.8). Here we might note once again in particular 4.5–7, where the coming of the Spirit into the heart is what establishes the common bond of sonship. From the close parallel in Rom. 8.15–17 it is evident that the experience of Spirit and of sonship was understood as part of the common heritage shared by all who wanted to identify with Jesus and as marking them out as his. The verb used in both cases (Rom.

---

[51] 'This reception of the "Spirit" is the primary datum of the Christian churches in Galatian', H. D. Betz, 'Spirit, Freedom and Law. Paul's Message to the Galatian Churches', *SEA* 39 (1974) pp. 145–60, here 146; see also D. J. Lull, *The Spirit in Galatia* (SBLDS 49; Chico: Scholars Press, 1978).

8.15; Gal. 4.6) also indicates the peculiar intensity of this shared experience – the Spirit's crying, 'Abba! Father!'.[52]

It is equally important to note that such reception of the Spirit was part of the expectation widely shared within Judaism at large. The hope of such an outpouring of the Spirit was a feature of several notable prophecies regarding the age to come (e.g. Isa. 32.15; Ezek. 37.4–14; Joel 2.28–9), and the Qumran community had already been making similar claims to experience the eschatological Spirit.[53] Paul was able to build on this part of the shared heritage by identifying the promised Spirit with the blessing promised to and through Abraham (3.14). Likewise, if Acts 2 is anything to go by, there was a common perception among the first Christian Jews that their own participation in the new age had been marked by the outpouring of the Spirit at Pentecost. Certainly Paul was able to assume elsewhere that the experience of the Spirit was the fundamental defining feature of the Christian without any suggestion that he was making a controversial claim (e.g. Rom. 8.9, 14; 1 Cor. 2.12; 12.13).

The Spirit was thus an integral part of the web of shared convictions and experiences. As just indicated, it could be seen as a climax to the story of Israel and mark out personal participation in the apocalyptic transition from old world to new creation. Moreover, reception of the Spirit was the other side of the act of faith with which participation in the new creation could be said to have began (3.2, 5, 14; note also 5.5–6 and 22).[54] Most striking of all, the experience of the Spirit in some degree recapitulated the story of Christ: it came in response to faith exercised in the crucified Christ (3.1–2); and it reproduced the same spirit of sonship in the believer (4.5–7). It is this last feature which enables us to give a little more definition to the experience of the Spirit as understood by Paul and other very early Christians: not just as experience of surging

---

[52] The verb *krazon* ('crying'), as in Rom. 8.15, indicates a cry of some intensity (cf. BAGD, *krazo*).

[53] E.g. 1QS 4.21; CD 2.12; 1QH 12.12; 14.13; 16.12.

[54] As has been recently noted by S. K. Williams, 'Justification and the Spirit in Galatians', *JSNT* 29 (1987) pp. 91–100, the experience of the Spirit and the status of justification were for Paul (but also more widely) two sides of the same coin.

emotions (cf. Rom. 5.5; 1 Thess. 1.6), or of charismatic empowering (as in Gal. 3.5), or of inspired utterance (as in 1 Cor. 14), or of ecstatic experience (cf. Acts 2.4; 1 Cor. 12.2; 14.12), but as experience patterned on Christ's (cf. 4.19) and as conforming to Christ's sonship (4.6–7). It is precisely as the Spirit of the Son (4.6) that Paul expected the Spirit to be known and acknowledged within the churches.[55]

Here too, of course, matters of controversy soon gathered about the shared experience. What should follow from this shared experience of the Spirit on the basis of the shared experience of believing (3.3)? Was the blessing of Abraham summed up in the Spirit given so directly and without further qualification to Gentiles? What difference did identification of the Spirit as the Spirit of Christ make to traditional Jewish understanding of the Spirit given by God?[56] The fact that Paul could pose the apocalyptic antithesis as between Spirit and flesh (5.16–25) was one thing, but the implication of 4.29 that ethnic Israel belonged to the wrong side of the antithesis could not but be profoundly disturbing for most of Paul's fellow Christian Jews. Once again, then, there are matters which require further clarification. For the moment, however, we can simply note that the experience of the Spirit was part of the common foundation and presupposition shared by the first Christians.

The theological significance of all this is already evident: the assumption that life should be determined by stories from another age, that the story of a historical individual can have such profound consequences for later generations, that life should be lived from the conviction that a decisive shift in reality has taken place; the appeal to experience of an otherly power from without, the integration of rational message and

---

[55] The understanding of the Spirit as the Spirit of Christ is common to different strands of the NT (Acts 16.7; Rom. 8.9; Gal. 4.6; Phil. 1.19; 1 Pet. 1.11), and reflects a common perception within first-century Christianity that Christ (the character of Christ as remembered in the Jesus tradition and proclaimed in the gospel of the cross) provided a means of discerning and defining the Spirit; see my *Jesus and the Spirit*, ch. 10.

[56] It is a striking fact that Paul never ascribes to Christ the giving of the Spirit, only to God (1 Cor. 2.12; 2 Cor. 1.21–2; 5.5; Gal. 4.6; 1 Thess. 4.8; also Eph. 1.17).

non-rational experience, faith as trustful openness to this message and power. The simple fact is that such was the ground and constitution of earliest Christian claims; it was such beliefs confirmed by such experiences which gave Christianity its initial power and impact in individual transformation and social bonding as it began to spread round the eastern end of the Mediterranean. It was certainly these mutually recognized expressions of faith and impact of the Spirit which provided the basis for Paul's appeal to the Galatians and even to the other missionaries behind them.

As we move on to focus attention on the issues which divided Paul and the other missionaries and which are so much more prominent in this letter, therefore, we should not forget how extensive were the convictions and experiences which they shared and which remain the common basis of Christianity in all its continuing diversity, and how potent is the combination of belief and experience, of a faith which makes sense of experience and an experience which makes faith a living reality. We shall also see that Paul's main argument in Galatians is in effect an outworking of the shared convictions (chapter 4), while his exhortations regarding conduct are in effect a working out of the shared experience (chapter 5).

CHAPTER 4

The heritage of Abraham

In chapter 3 we concentrated on those features of the theology of Galatians which Paul held in common with his readers and other Christian Jews. Now we turn to the issues in dispute between Paul and the other missionaries. That is to say, we begin to investigate more closely the points at which Paul pressed beyond the shared convictions and experiences. Paul, of course, saw these points as integral to the shared convictions, as the inevitably corollary of the shared experiences. But evidently others, the other missionaries in particular, would have disputed that viewpoint, and with some vehemence.

What we are about to explore, therefore, are the points at which Paul was developing his own theology. Because of the canonical significance of the letter Christians have long since recognized these points as fundamental expressions of Christian faith. But we do well to realize that what we are about to look at was new theology, theology being freshly minted to meet the challenge of the occasion. In Galatians, as we noted at the beginning, we encounter theology in the making. Whether Paul had formulated these points before this we cannot tell. Certainly the degree to which they appear in Galatians as the response to the particular crisis in Galatia suggests that Paul was expressing himself in a new and forceful way. To repeat, he himself would not think of the points as innovative; for him they were simply a matter of spelling out the truth of the gospel and the significance of the cross. But in the history of Christian theology they appear in Galatians for the first time. And for the Galatians themselves, not to mention the other missionaries, their novel, not to say revolutionary character would no doubt have raised more than one pair of eyebrows.

In our exposition of the make or break issues and the fundamental agreements we have already indicated where the points of tension came between the shared assumptions of faith and the particular corollaries Paul sought to draw out. Clearly at the centre of everything was Paul's claim that his apostleship and gospel were for the Gentiles; that is what he had defended and advocated with such success at the Jerusalem council (2.1–10); that was what he felt compelled to defend afresh in this letter. It was this emergence of the Gentile question within the shared convictions and shared experiences which posed the questions. Given the axiomatic importance of the story of Israel, how were Gentiles to be incorporated into it? How could Paul claim that his gospel was in continuity with that story? How could Gentiles come to share in the heritage of Abraham? Given the importance of the story of the Christ, did it modify or transform the story of Israel? What was the significance of the cross for this central issue? Given not least the apocalyptic shift marked by Christ and the cross, did they not wholly relativize the claims and presumptions of all who lived within the old age, Jews included? Given the importance of faith in this Christ, how did that affect the older understanding of the relation between God and the descendants of Abraham, particularly as characterized by the law? Given the importance of the shared Spirit, what was its significance for the central issue? Was it enough to say that it embodied the blessing of Abraham? Was it only as the Spirit of Christ that the Spirit of God fulfilled the prophetic hopes for the age to come? How did the apocalyptic tension between Spirit and flesh relate to the Gentile claim to participation in the heritage of Abraham?

These are the issues which lie behind the main thrust of Paul's argument in the central section of his letter (chapters 3 and 4). The simplest way to proceed is to highlight the main themes of that argument without becoming clogged in the fine detail. However, since he prepares the ground and already hints at its contours in chapters 1 and 2, we will have to include the main points to emerge from them in the analysis and to draw out the fuller significance which Paul saw in the convictions and experiences he shared with his fellow Christian Jews.

THE SIGNIFICANCE OF PAUL'S CONVERSION

Since Paul takes such pains to give his own personal testimony (1.13–2.21) as prolegomenon to his main argument, it is important to note where he begins that testimony, for in his own mind and in the rhetoric of the letter itself that point marks also the beginning of his own distinct story as a Christian and thus also the beginning of his own distinctive theology.

From persecutor to apostle

Paul begins by reminding his readers of how he himself had been a prime exponent and practitioner of Judaism.

For you have heard of my way of life previously in Judaism, that in excessive measure I persecuted the church of God and tried to destroy it; and that I progressed in Judaism beyond many of my contemporaries among my people, being exceedingly zealous for the traditions of my fathers. (1.13–14)

Paul is making several points to the Galatians here. One is that he himself knew from inside the life-style and commitment which they were finding so attractive; if Judaism was so enticing, particularly Jewish customs and traditions, then he himself had been more committed to this Judaism and more successful in it than many (= most?) of his contemporaries. When he would subsequently seek to dissuade the Galatians from making such commitment and embracing such traditions, it was not because he was ignorant of their appeal. Another is the clear indication that it was this same commitment which had made him an enemy of the church: it was as an expression of his way of life within Judaism that he persecuted the church in excessive measure and tried to destroy it.[1] Again the impli-

---

[1] Paul may have had in mind only(!) the disciplinary flogging (up to 39 lashes) indicated in 2 Cor. 11.24 (see e.g. A. Hultgren, 'Paul's Pre-Christian Persecution of the Church', *JBL* 95 (1976) pp. 97–111), but the language and precedents (of such zeal – see below) indicate considerable violence.

cation is obvious: there was something antipathetical between the typical and traditional life-style practised within Judaism and the church of God.

The theological logic behind this is hinted at in the phrase 'being exceedingly zealous for the traditions of my fathers'. That Paul was talking of his zeal also as a persecutor is as clearly implied here as it is explicit in Paul's other piece of self-testimony later on (Phil. 3.6 – 'as to zeal, a persecutor of the church'). Why 'zeal' should mean persecution becomes clear when we recall the history of zeal within Jewish tradition, which treasured the memory of several ideal types of zeal. Simeon and Levi had acted out of such zeal when they expunged the defilement of their sister Dinah by destroying the Shechemites (Judith 9.2–4; *Jub.* 30.5–20; referring to Gen. 34). Particularly significant in later perspective was the action of Phinehas, who, out of his deep zeal, killed the Israelite who had taken a Midianite woman, thus making atonement for the people of Israel (Num. 25.6–13; Sir. 45.23–4; 1 Macc. 2.54).[2] When the zeal of Elijah was celebrated within the same context, the implication is that what was in mind was his slaughtering of the prophets of Baal after defeating them in the contest on Mount Carmel (Sir. 48.2; 1 Macc. 2.58; referring particularly to 1 Kings 18.40). And it is explicitly stated that Mattathias started the Maccabean revolt when, burning with zeal, like Phinehas of old, he cut down the Syrian official and the apostate Jew who dared to offer a Gentile sacrifice (1 Macc. 2.15–28).

The common denominator in all these episodes is the same: a zeal to maintain Israel's distinctiveness over against other peoples, a zeal which resisted sexual relations across the ethnic divide, and which absolutely refused any compromise with other religions or attempt at syncretistic dilution of Israel's unique relation with God; and a zeal which was prepared to use force to maintain this distinctiveness. This zeal, in fact, was understood simply as the corollary to the zeal of the Lord for Israel. God had chosen Israel for himself, and he was jealous/

---

[2] For the significance of Phinehas in Jewish tradition see M. Hengel, *The Zealots* (Edinburgh: T. & T. Clark, 1989) pp. 149–77.

zealous (it is the same word in Hebrew and Greek) over them; that was why Israel must worship no other gods (Exod. 20.5; 34.14; Deut. 6.14–15). Phinehas' zeal/jealousy was lauded precisely as an expression of God's zeal/jealousy over Israel (Num. 25.11–13). In short, for anyone familiar with the Jewish tradition of zeal, zeal denoted determined and forceful resistance to anything which or any who were compromising or threatening the distinctiveness of Israel's covenant relation with God, fellow Jews not least.

Within the context of the traditions of the fathers, Paul's own zeal and the reason why it found expression in persecution of the church become clear. It must be because Paul saw the church as threatening the distinctiveness of Israel's covenant calling and status. Why that should be so is also fairly obvious – because the church was already opening the door to Gentiles (Acts 11.20). That is, Christian Jews were accepting into membership of their (Jewish) sect Gentiles, without, it would appear, requiring of them commitment to Judaism in the traditional terms – circumcision and observance of the law.

This seems to be confirmed by the way Paul describes his conversion (1.15–16). Not as a conversion as such, but as a calling – a commissioning, as already noted, to take the gospel to the Gentiles. As Paul looked back to the beginning of his Christian experience he was in absolutely no doubt that the commission to take the gospel to the Gentiles had been given him from the first, and that this was a necessary and inevitable implication of the revelation of Christ, to him personally (1.11–12, 16). How soon the theological ramifications of the Damascus experience became clear to him we cannot now tell. At least we can deduce that he was converted to the position he had just been seeking to persecute; that is, from being one determined to prevent fellow Jews from undermining Israel's distinctive covenant relation with God through admission of Gentiles to the church, he became one as eager as they to take the good news of Jesus to the Gentiles.[3] But did he already see

---

[3] This double aspect of Paul's conversion/prophetic commissioning is not given enough weight by K. O. Sandnes, *Paul – One of the Prophets?* (WUNT 2.43; Tüb-

this as part of the apocalyptic shift in the ages, and did he at once think through the implications of this apocalyptic perspective for the traditional claims for Israel's distinctiveness?[4] We cannot tell. It must suffice to note that Galatians itself provides the first clear exposition of these implications known to us, and it is likely that several of its lines of argument must have come as a severe shock to other Christian Jews.

In sum, then, the new growing point in Paul's theology, which emerged for him directly from his encounter with the risen Christ on the Damascus road, was that the old self-understanding of Judaism, of which he had been an arch exponent, must be revised. A Judaism characterized by the zeal to keep the boundaries between Jew and Gentile clearly drawn must be replaced by the commission to preach Messiah Jesus among the Gentiles, with the implication (not yet fully thought through) that Gentiles who received this good news could be accepted into membership of the church without requiring that they become proselytes.

The Jerusalem consultation

The emergence of a circumcision-free gospel on the part of Christian Jews is a wholly remarkable event in religious history – passed over virtually in silence by both Paul here and Acts 11.20. It would also be helpful to know whether Paul began to preach to Gentiles immediately (in Arabia – 1.17); but on this issue no certainty can be achieved.[5] For an analysis of the theology of Galatians itself, however, it is sufficient to note that prior to the Jerusalem consultation Paul had been preaching to

ingen: Mohr, 1991) pp. 56–69, and M. A. Seifrid, *Justification by Faith. The Origin and Development of a Central Pauline Theme* (SNT 68; Leiden: Brill, 1992) pp. 152–71.

[4] In the traditional Jewish eschatological schema the nations either were destroyed or subjugated, or became pilgrims and proselytes to Zion; see e.g. E. P. Sanders, *Jesus and Judaism* (London: SCM, 1985) pp. 213–18.

[5] Those who think that Paul went to Arabia to preach include Betz, *Galatians* pp. 73–4; Bruce, *Galatians* p. 96; and C. K. Barrett, *Freedom and Obligation. A Study of the Epistle to the Galatians* (London: SPCK, 1985) p. 8. H. M. Schenke suggests Petra in particular, 'Four Problems in the Life of Paul Reconsidered', *The Future of Early Christianity. Essays in Honor of H. Koester*, ed. B. A. Pearson (Minneapolis: Fortress Press, 1991) pp. 319–28, here 323.

Gentiles for some time (as a missionary of the church at Antioch), and that the church at Antioch and its daughter churches accepted Gentiles as members (by baptism in the name of Jesus Christ) without requiring them to be circumcised.

How it was that Christian Jews felt able thus to disregard the explicit injunctions of Gen. 17.9–14 is one of the great unsolved mysteries of Christianity's beginnings. Some Jews may have regarded Gentiles as acceptable to God on other terms, outside the covenant signified by circumcision and documented by law.[6] This is unlikely in the case of those who had shared Paul's previous attitude (1.13–14). For if we are right, Paul engaged in violent persecution of his fellow Jews precisely because he saw their acceptance of Gentiles as a threat to Israel's distinct-iveness as God's own elect people. Moreover, as already noted, the self-identity of the new Jesus movement as 'the church of God' (1.13) constituted a claim to direct continuity with the assembly of Israel. The only obvious alternative is to assume that more traditionally minded Christian Jews saw the accept-ance of uncircumcised Gentiles as exceptional or anomalous and regarded them somewhat as God-fearers on the way to full proselyte status.[7]

The picture begins to become clearer at the Jerusalem council, where Paul's advocacy that Gentiles be recognized as also belonging to Christ won the day. There was a significant faction ('false brothers', 2.4) who tried to insist on circumcision as an unbreakable *sine qua non* – they at least could understand acceptance of Gentiles only in terms of their becoming prose-lytes – and Paul makes no attempt to hide his complete antipa-thy towards them.[8] What is most striking, however, is that, in the event, the leadership of the Jerusalem church gave their clear backing to Paul (2.6–9). Once again we should note how

---

[6] See particularly P. Fredriksen, 'Judaism, the Circumcision of Gentiles, and Apoca-lyptic Hope: Another Look at Galatians 1 and 2', *JTS* 42 (1991) pp. 532–64, here 548–58.

[7] Cf. particularly Juvenal, *Satires* 14.96–106, who indicates what must have been a fairly common pattern in first-century Rome itself: the son of the God-fearing father in due course becomes a proselyte.

[8] Note the language he uses – 'false brothers', 'smuggled in', 'sneaked in', 'spy out', 'in order that they might enslave us' (2.4).

astonishing a step that was: that the now significant numbers of Gentile converts should be accepted as fellow followers of the way, itself a sect within Judaism, without requiring circumcision, the universally recognized mark of Judaism, and even though the issue had come out in open debate involving conservative James – this was indeed a decision of epochal significance for the emergence of Christianity. In this case the justification was clear – the manifest success of Paul's mission, the same demonstration of grace and Spirit in Paul's Gentile converts as in those Jews won to the faith by Peter (2.7–9). The power of the living experience of grace overcame the force of ancient sacred tradition.

The issue, however, had been by no means wholly clarified or closed. The Jerusalem agreement was probably something of a compromise which masked a variety of understandings of what had been actually agreed. The 'false brothers' presumably would have been little reconciled to the agreement. More important, some of the Jerusalem leadership, probably including James, seem to have understood the decision regarding Titus still as exceptional rather than as establishing a new pattern for relationship between God and believers and between believers. This is suggested by the urging of the Jerusalem leaders that Paul should remember the poor (2.10). For active concern for the poor was a particular and distinctive feature of Jewish law and tradition,[9] and alms-giving was widely understood within Judaism as an essential obligation of membership of the covenant people.[10] The effect of this addendum to the Jerusalem agreement, therefore, was to reinforce the distinctively Jewish sense of covenant obligation. That circumcision was not necessary had been conceded; otherwise the traditional obligations of the law of the covenant should be maintained.

In short, the full implications for Christian Jewish self-

---

[9] E.g. Deut. 24.10–22; Pss. 10.2, 9; 12.5; 14.6 etc.; Isa. 3.14–15; 10.1–2; 58.6–7; Amos 8.4–6.

[10] Dan. 4.27; Sir. 3.30; 29.12; 40.24; Tob. 4.10; 12.9; 14.11; see further G. Schrenk, *dikaiosune*, *TDNT* 2.196; K. Berger, 'Almosen für Israel: zum historischen Kontext der paulinischen Kollekte', *NTS* 23 (1976–7) pp. 180–204, here 183–92.

understanding of admitting Gentiles so freely into a Jewish sect were still not clear. How the Gentile issue was to be understood in the light of the gospel, in the light of the apocalyptic significance of the story of Jesus and the cross, in the light of faith in Messiah Jesus and the outpouring of the Spirit, had not yet been fully addressed. Paul himself may have been already clear that a fairly radical revision was required of the self-understanding of the people of God and its defining boundaries. But in the event, the issue only came fully into the open in the incident at Antioch.

THE SIGNIFICANCE OF THE ANTIOCH INCIDENT

The significance of the Antioch incident (2.11–14) for Paul's theology has not been given sufficient recognition in the history of interpretation of Galatians. It can be highlighted in two ways. As already noted,[11] it is likely that Paul lost out in his confrontation with Peter at Antioch, and that the result was a breach with Antioch, with the Jerusalem leadership and even with his previous colleague Barnabas. The incident at Antioch therefore marks the emergence of Paul's distinct emphases – the theological emphases which occasioned both the confrontation itself (2.11, 14) and Paul's consequent isolation. That is to say, the Antioch incident marks the beginning of the explicitly distinctive features of Paul's theology. Not of his theology as a whole, for, as we have seen, so much of that was shared with his fellow Christian Jews. Nor of the distinctive claims which he had maintained with success at the Jerusalem meeting (2.2, 6–9). Nor indeed of what Paul evidently already regarded as the obvious outworking of his gospel (the situation which had prevailed in the Antioch church before the coming of the group from James). But certainly at Antioch issues which had been submerged till then came to the surface, and Paul in speaking to them evidently found himself a lone voice, maintaining a theological interpretation of shared convictions which proved unacceptable to his fellow Christian Jews. If

[11] See above pp. 13–14.

then we look for the distinctive theology of Paul as found in Galatians we cannot avoid focusing on the Antioch incident.

Rhetorical analysis of the letter has also underlined the importance of the Antioch incident. For Paul does not end his autobiographical narrative with his success at Jerusalem. He evidently felt it necessary to go on to his much less successful encounter at Antioch. The implication is that in the letter he would try to retrieve the failure at Antioch and re-establish the success at Jerusalem. As already noted, Paul does not round off his description of the incident but merges his response to Peter into the opening statement of his appeal to the Galatians (2.15–21). The challenge which he addresses in Galatians is the challenge he failed to meet at Antioch – how can Christian Jews compel the Gentiles to judaize (2.14)?[12] Galatians is what he should have said to Peter at Antioch had time and sufficient reflection allowed it.[13]

The issue posed

It is the Antioch incident which shows just how little clarity had been achieved at the Jerusalem consultation. Those who came from James, that is, claiming, explicitly or implicity, the authority of James, had obviously been distressed by the free association between Christian Jews (including Peter) and Gentiles at Antioch (2.12). Whatever the precise character of that table-fellowship,[14] the issue was clear: maintenance of the food laws and avoidance of 'the food of Gentiles' had always been points of particular sensitivity for conscientious Jews (e.g. 1 Macc. 1.62–3; Dan. 1.8–16; Tobit 1.10–13); in the eyes of the incomers from James, the Christian Jews had been failing these obligations under the law, and thus compromising their status as God's covenant people. To be more precise, the issue was the failure of the Christian Jews to maintain that separation from

---

[12] See above p. 15 n. 26.

[13] J. Bligh, *Galatians* (London: St Paul, 1969) pp. 235–6, argues the implausible thesis that 'St Paul's Antioch Discourse' not only extended through 2.21, but through to 5.10 plus 6.16–18 (minus 4.11–20).

[14] See my 'The Incident at Antioch (Gal. 2.11–18)', in *Jesus, Paul and the Law* pp. 129–82, with further clarification in my *Galatians* at 2.12.

Gentiles which marked out the Jews as set apart to God. This is clearly indicated in the way Paul tells the story: before the coming of the group from James Peter 'had eaten with the Gentiles' (2.12); thereafter he withdrew and 'separated himself' from them (2.12);[15] in the eyes of the James' group Peter had been 'living like a Gentile and not as a Jew' (2.14); he had been behaving like 'Gentile sinners' (2.15).[16] Despite the Jerusalem agreement the consequences of Gentile acceptance of the gospel for Jewish claims to a distinctive relation with God had been neither thought through nor agreed.

The implications of the last charge (behaving like Gentile sinners) are particularly revealing and serious. For 'sinners' by definition were excluded from the blessings of the covenant;[17] that was why many Jews regarded Gentiles as 'sinners' by definition, as here.[18] And such accusation was not untypical of intra-Jewish polemic, with one faction, confident that it understood and sought to practise the law correctly, more than ready to condemn other factions as 'sinners', whose conduct put them outside the covenant.[19] This was the seriousness of the Antioch incident: that Gentile converts were being seen as a threat to Jewish covenant status and hope of salvation; that association of Christian Jews and Christian Gentiles was being seen not as drawing Gentiles within the sphere of covenant righteousness, but as causing Jews to be accounted sinners along with the Gentiles.

It was against this attitude that Paul rebelled. The fact that Christ had accepted these Gentiles in the same way (believed in him, baptized in his name, received his Spirit) should be

[15] Since Paul had been a Pharisee, and since 'Pharisee' is normally taken as originally a nickname meaning 'the separated ones', it may well be that Paul intended a pun here: Peter 'played the Pharisee'.

[16] This phrase hardly expresses Paul's own view of Gentiles (cf. 2.17), and should probably be heard as an echo of what the group from James had said in their criticism of Peter's eating with Gentiles. See my 'Echoes of Intra-Jewish Polemic in Paul's Letter to the Galatians', *JBL* 112 (1993).

[17] E.g. Exod. 32.33; Deut. 29.18; Pss. 1.4–6; 92.7; Sir. 9.11–12; 1QS 2.5–18; *Pss. Sol.* 15.10–13. See also D. A. Neale, *None But the Sinners. Religious Categories in the Gospel of Luke* (JSNTS 58; Sheffield Academic, 1991) ch. 3.

[18] Ps. 9.17; Tobit 13.6; *Jub.* 23.23–4; *Pss. Sol.* 2.1–2; Matt. 5.47/Luke 6.33.

[19] E.g. 1 Macc. 1.34; 2.44, 48; *1 Enoch* 5.4–7; 82.4–5; 1QH 2.8–12; 1QpHab. 5.4–8; *Pss. Sol.* 4.8; 13.6–12.

sufficient ground for Christian Jews to accept them also in table-fellowship. To count Christian Jews who thus joined with Christian Gentiles as 'sinners' was tantamount to making the Christ who accepted both the 'servant of sin' – an impossible thought (2.17). It is not possible to deduce with confidence that Paul at this point had in mind the tradition of Jesus' own table-fellowship with 'sinners' (Mark 2.16; Matt. 11.19/Luke 7.34), but the protest against excluding others as 'sinners' from the grace of God is the same, and the allusion to Jesus as 'servant/waiter' should probably be recognized as a graceful allusion to a tradition familiar to both recipients and author (Luke 22.27 pars).[20]

The issue here between Paul and the other Christian Jews at Antioch, and now at Galatia, comes to clearest focus in 2.16.

Not by works of the law

It is fairly obvious from 2.16 that the attitude against which Paul was protesting is summed up in the phrase 'works of the law'. It was the attitude which maintained the separation of Jew from Gentile as a matter of principle. It was the attitude which counted Gentiles and those who associated with them as 'sinners' (to be noted is the fact that the two references to 'sinners', in 2.15 and 17, bracket 2.16). The heart of Paul's appeal to Peter was to their shared knowledge that 'no human being is justified by works of the law but only through faith in Jesus Christ'. That is to say, the appeal was to their shared experience of faith ('through faith in Christ') against the conduct which had divided them at Antioch (not 'by works of the law').

What then does Paul mean by 'works of the law'? Traditionally the phrase has been taken to denote human achievement, the presumption that by one's own effort salvation could be achieved or earned. The denial of such possibility is certainly a valid theological insight of fundamental importance. And to see that theological principle as summed up in our

---

[20] See further below p. 117.

phrase has a certain plausibility – works of the law as a particularly Jewish attempt to achieve God's acceptance by obeying the law. The problem is that the attitude is not particularly Jewish. Directly to the contrary, Jewish theology began from the recognition that God had chosen an insignificant and pretty worthless slave people, had rescued them from their slavery, and made his covenant with them. It was nothing they had achieved or earned, neither could achieve it, nor needed to earn it; it was a matter of grace from the start.[21]

The same point emerges when we consider Paul's theology of righteousness. For his talk of righteousness derives directly from the Old Testament, as his two most famous OT quotations illustrate (3.6 – Gen. 15.6; 3.11 – Hab. 2.4). And in Jewish theology righteousness as between God and human beings is a covenant category – righteousness as the meeting of the obligations laid upon each party by the covenant relationship.[22] For the Psalmist and Second Isaiah in particular that meant especially the obligation God had accepted when he first chose Israel, the obligation to preserve and save Israel when things went wrong.[23] Here too what later theology calls 'the prevenience of grace' was fundamental to Jewish self-understanding of the covenant relationship between God and Israel. It is in this sense that we can recognize Paul's doctrine of 'justification by faith' to be a thoroughly Jewish doctrine. The Christian specific, 'by faith in Christ Jesus', did not mark any fundamental shift on this point in the thinking of Paul the Jew or Peter the Jew.

What of the law? We shall attempt to clarify the role of the law more fully later. Here we need simply note that in Jewish theology the law was given not as a means to gain righteousness, but as a means of living righteously. In two senses, of

---

[21] See e.g. the basic theological structure of such fundamental statements as Exod. 20.1–2 and Deut. 7.6–11. To remind us of this basic character of Israel's religion has been one of the principal contributions of E. P. Sanders, *Paul and Palestinian Judaism* (London: SCM, 1977), index 'grace'; also *Judaism: Practice and Belief 63 BCE–66 CE* (London: SCM, 1992) pp. 262–78.

[22] Too much neglected have been the excellent summary treatments of E. R. and P. J. Achtemeier in *IDB* 4.80–5, 91–9.

[23] See above p. 39.

which Deuteronomy provides classic expression. First, the law was given as part of the covenant the God of Israel made with his people: having chosen and rescued Israel from slavery, God gave the law to show how life should be lived within the covenant, what he required of members of his covenant people. And second, the law was given to provide through its sacrificial system a means of atonement for sin. The suggestion, still often heard, that the law required perfect obedience and that nothing less would suffice, completely ignores the fact that the possibility of repentance and the provision of atonement have been prominent features of Jewish theology and practice from the first.

What then of 'works of the law'? The preceding paragraphs indicate clearly enough that the traditional interpretation of 'works of the law' as self-achieved righteousness makes no sense against the background of classic Jewish theology. More to the point, it hardly fits the present context in Galatians (2.16), where thought of self-achieved righteousness would skew the thought completely from the issue posed by the Antioch incident. In contrast, a much more obvious meaning emerges when we mesh the theology presupposed by the James' group in the Antioch incident with the covenantal theology just sketched above.

An obvious meaning for the phrase 'works of the law', then, is the human activities required by the law *of those within the covenant*.[24] In terms of the above sketch of Jewish theology, works of the law arė what God expects of the people he has chosen as his own, the obligations which membership of God's covenant people placed upon them. But that included the obligation to maintain Israel's distinctiveness from the other peoples not chosen by God. To live as God's people was to live

---

[24] Cf. J. B. Tyson, '"Works of Law" in Galatians', *JBL* 92 (1973) pp. 423–31; M. Bachmann, *Sünder oder Übertreter. Studien zur Argumentation in Gal. 2.15ff.* (WUNT 59; Tübingen: Mohr, 1992) pp. 90–100. The phrase introduced by Sanders (n. 21 above), 'covenantal nomism', is a good modern equivalent to 'works of the law'. For a further presentation of this understanding of 'works of the law', in dialogue with others, see my 'Yet Once More – "The Works of the Law". A Response', *JSNT* 46 (1992) pp. 99–117.

precisely in a manner which would show them to be different from other peoples. In the words of Philo, for example they were to be a people 'which shall dwell alone, not reckoned among other nations ... because in virtue of the distinction of their peculiar customs they do not mix with others to depart from the ways of their fathers' (*Mos.* 1.278).[25] It was precisely this sense of distinctiveness and thus also of set-apartness which obviously lay behind the attitude of the James' group. And the fact that Peter and Barnabas found it impossible to stand out against that same attitude simply shows how deeply rooted and widespread within Jewish thinking it must have been. In typically Jewish thought to do the works of the law would mean maintaining a social life as far as practically possible apart from Gentiles.[26]

It is equally obvious why the issue should come to focus in the table-fellowship at Antioch. For it was precisely in the social setting of the shared meal that Jewish distinctiveness would be most threatened: as already noted, maintenance of the food laws and avoidance of 'the food of Gentiles' had always been points of sensitivity for conscientious Jews; the talk of 'separation' (2.12) echoes the similar concern of Pharisees to separate themselves from other Jews in the matter of food; and again as already noted, the repeated talk of 'sinners' recalls the similar criticism of Jesus for eating with 'sinners'.[27] For many Jews, then, the practice of the law, the works of the law, which most clearly maintained covenant distinctiveness from other peoples in the practicalities of daily life were those which governed table-fellowship.[28] And for Jews with a more restricted or sectarian understanding of covenant righteousness, works of the law would include particularly those which most

---

[25] See further my *Romans* (WBC 38; Dallas: Word, 1988) pp. lxix–lxx.
[26] Cf. particularly E. P. Sanders, 'Jewish Association with Gentiles and Galatians 2.11–14', *Studies in Paul and John. In Honor of J. L. Martyn*, ed. R. T. Fortna & B. R. Gaventa (Nashville: Abingdon, 1990) pp. 170–88; P. J. Tomson, *Paul and the Jewish Law. Halakha in the Letters of the Apostle to the Gentiles* (Assen: Van Gorcum/Minneapolis: Fortress Press, 1990) pp. 226–36.
[27] See above p. 75.
[28] Cf. the other similar uses of 'eat with' in biblical Greek – Gen. 43.32; Ps. 100.5 LXX; Luke 15.2; Acts 10.41 and 11.3; 1 Cor. 5.11.

clearly documented and regulated the distinctiveness of their interpretation of the law.[29]

This then must be the reason why the issue posed at Antioch could be summed up in terms of 'works of the law'. The phrase epitomized the attitude which the group from James brought with them into the church at Antioch. Not a concern to earn salvation by good works. But a concern to maintain Israel's covenant obligations and distinctiveness, with the corollary, unavoidable so far as Peter and the others could see, that they must maintain separate tables from the Gentiles. It is this attitude to which Paul objects so fiercely in 2.16.

Through faith in Christ

His objection is summed up in the contrasting phrase – 'through faith in Jesus Christ'. His concern seems to have been to move Peter to the recognition that if 'faith in Christ' comes into conflict with 'works of the law', it is the former which must have the decisive weight. For he starts by appealing to their common acknowledgment that 'no human being is justified by works of the law but only (or except) through faith in Jesus Christ'.[30] But his implicit criticism of Peter was precisely that Peter *had* attempted to combine faith in Christ with maintenance of the works of the law which so excluded Gentiles. It was essential for Peter to realize, therefore, that faith in Christ alone was sufficient, that it overruled any need to rely on works of the law. Indeed, the fact that works of the law could come into conflict with faith in Christ, as in the Antioch incident, confirmed to Paul, had he not realized it earlier, that works of the law could be positively harmful. Thus he continues: 'so we have believed in Christ Jesus, in order that we might be justified by faith in Christ and *not* by works of the law, since by works of the law shall no flesh be justified'. Paul uses the

---

[29] This was so certainly at Qumran, whose scrolls have provided the only close parallel to Paul's phrase (4QFlor. 1.7; 4QMMT; 1QS 5.21, 23; 6.18).

[30] Whatever the precise force of *ean me* ('but only'), the basic fact remains that Paul sought to move Peter away from a 'faith plus works' praxis to a 'faith only' understanding. See also my *Jesus, Paul and the Law* p. 212.

purpose clause deliberately to bring out the full significance of their own believing in Christ. The fact that faith in Christ was sufficient for Jews and Gentiles to be accepted by the Lord Jesus Christ can now be seen to have the fuller purpose of attesting that faith alone is sufficient, and that continued adherence to works of the law on the part of Christian Jews is both unnecessary and itself a threat to the sufficiency of that faith.

The same point is reinforced in the snatch of personal testimony with which Paul rounds off the summary statement leading in to his main argument (2.18–21). 'I through the law have died to the law, in order that I may live for God ... And the life I now live in the flesh, I live by the faith which is in the son of God ... who gave himself for me' (2.19–20). What Paul means by his 'dying to the law' is not clear. He evidently had in mind his own (typical) transition from old age to new (cf. 1.4; 6.14–15). What this says about the law is something we will attempt to clarify shortly. Even more obscure is what Paul meant by saying 'I died to the law through the law'. By 'through the law' he could have referred to his law-inspired zeal to persecute the church which brought him face to face with the risen Christ (1.13–14), or to his self-identification with Christ's death ('I have been crucified with Christ', 2.19) under the curse of the law (3.13), or to the law's transitional role prior to the coming of Christ (3.19–4.7). These are questions which we will be able to clarify to some extent as the analysis proceeds. For the moment it is sufficient to note the contrast which Paul's formulation makes between law and faith. In coming to faith in Christ he had died to the law. In context, that must at least include life lived in terms of the works of the law. The law, explicitly as understood and practised within the Judaism which Paul had left behind, the works of the law, had proved itself as undermining the relation with Christ established through faith and thus as an alternative and even opponent to faith.

These are the points, the sufficiency of faith and what that means for Christian Jewish understanding of the law, which Paul goes on to develop more explicitly and to emphasize more strongly in the course of the main argument itself.

THE SUFFICIENCY OF FAITH

The theme of faith/believing occurs more intensively in Gal. 3 than in any other chapter of the New Testament, with the exception of Rom. 4 and Heb. 11. Gal. 3, then, is one of the great sources for a theological understanding of faith, Paul's first full-scale attempt, so far as our evidence goes, to explain why faith in Christ is so important, and particularly for traditional Jewish self-understanding.

Abraham as type and progenitor

Having recalled his readers to their own foundational experience of gospel, faith and Spirit (3.1–5),[31] Paul makes the first decisive link to Israel's sacred history – 'Just as "Abraham believed God, and it was reckoned to him for righteousness"' (3.6 – citing Gen. 15.6). The appeal to Abraham was well chosen. For Abraham was generally regarded as the father of the Jewish people (e.g. Isa. 51.2; Matt. 3.9). And Abraham was commonly seen within Jewish circles as the model of the devout Jew: 'perfect in all of his actions with the Lord' (*Jub.* 23.10); 'a friend of God because he kept the commandments of God' (CD 3.2). Perhaps more to the point here, he was remembered as in effect the first proselyte and type of true conversion (e.g. Philo, *Abraham* 60–88; Josephus, *Ant.* 1.155; *Apoc. Abr.* 1–8).

Moreover, Gen. 15.6 naturally functioned within this portrayal of Abraham. As 1 Macc. 2.52 and James 2.23 indicate, Abraham's faith was interpreted in terms of his faithfulness (same word; cf. 3.9) in his offering up of Isaac at God's command (cf. Sir. 44.19–21; *Jub.* 17.15–18). Paul, however, does not seem to have been concerned to counter this line of interpretation. Perhaps because the focus of the controversy occasioned by the other missionaries was more on the issue of circumcision (that is on Gen. 17 rather than on Gen. 22). But

---

[31] See above pp. 59–63.

the primary reason must be that Paul was confident that his Galatian audiences would identify with Abraham in his believing, and understand Abraham's experience and act of faith in the light of their own. Hence the 'just as' at the beginning of 3.6. As with Abraham, so with the Galatians, it is trustful belief which constitutes the righteousness for which God looks, the life acceptable to God.

For the same reason Paul can draw as an immediate corollary from the citation of Gen. 15.6, that 'those of faith, they are Abraham's sons' (3.7). It should be self-evident to the Galatians that the faith which had brought them the Spirit was the same faith which had brought Abraham righteousness. The corollary shows Paul's awareness of the context of Gen. 15.6 – that what Abraham believed was the promise of offspring (Gen. 15.4–6). He thus makes bold to deduce that the faith which received that promise also indicates the character of Abraham's offspring. Since it was faith which thus established the covenant relation with God, the same faith would be the distinctive characteristic of those who shared in the covenant relation thus established with Abraham – those of faith are those who inherit the covenant relation established through Abraham's believing. Since Abraham could be regarded as the first proselyte and model for true conversion, it followed that the means by which Abraham received right standing with God applied to all coming to faith from outside Judaism. Paul may also be playing on the characteristic semitic idiom which uses 'son of' to denote a share in a particular quality (son of wisdom = a wise man); so, 'son of Abraham' means a person who shared Abraham's faith. At all events, the point Paul is making is clear: that as with Abraham, faith alone is sufficient for God's full acceptance.

To make his case for linking Abraham with believing Gentiles Paul did not need to depend solely on his appeal to the Galatians' own experience of faith. For the Abraham story itself makes clear that the promise to Abraham of offspring included also the promise of blessing to the nations – 'In you all the nations shall be blessed' (3.8). The wording is derived from both Gen. 12.3 and 18.18, but reflects a sustained theme within the patriarchal narratives (Gen. 22.17–18; 26.4; 28.14). In other words, the divine intention to extend the blessing enjoyed by Abraham to the nations/Gentiles was explicit from the beginning. Significantly, Paul calls this promise an early proclamation of the gospel, and again indicates that God's eschatological acceptance of the Gentiles by faith was at the heart of the gospel for Paul – 'scripture, foreseeing that God would justify the Gentiles from faith preached the gospel beforehand to Abraham' (3.8). And thus he can conclude: 'Consequently those of faith [Galatian Gentile converts not least] are blessed with faithful Abraham' (3.9).

The argument here could not be more fundamental to Paul's understanding of the gospel. So far as he was concerned, the story of Abraham established two crucial points: first, that acceptance by God was a matter wholly and solely of faith on the human side; and, second, that integral to the covenant relation established with Abraham and his offspring was the divine intention to include the Gentiles within that blessing. On these two points Paul's gospel and distinctive theology rest entirely. Whatever clouded or undermined these two points went against the truth of the gospel.

The curse of the law

The paragraph which follows (3.10–14) seems to take the line of argument off at a tangent and is one of the most difficult to follow that Paul ever dictated. But as it contains rich theological meat we should attempt at least to grasp its main outline.

It is the opening sentence which throws commentators into confusion – 'For all who rely on works of the law are under a curse, for it is written, "Cursed is everyone who does not remain within all that has been written in the book of the law to do it"' (Deut. 27.26). The problem is how Paul can so casually and sweepingly indict his fellow Jews as 'under a curse'. The traditional answer has been that works of the law refer to human effort to keep the law, and since the law cannot be kept perfectly it is inevitable that all who so strive fall under its curse by reason of their failure.[32] But if what we have noted already is true, that will not do: 'works of the law' cannot be understood as a summary of human striving to achieve acceptance by God; and the Jewish system of law was designed precisely to deal with human failure through its sacrificial system.[33]

A more plausible answer is given by the context.[34] For one thing, Paul indicates that 3.10 begins an attempt to expound or explain (by means of the introductory 'for') the points just made. These were, we recall, that the gospel of justification *from faith, for Gentiles* was integral to the covenant promises given to Abraham from the beginning. It is immediately significant, then, that the subject of 3.10, 'as many as are from works of the law', is posed in obvious antithesis to the main subject of the preceding paragraph, 'those from faith' (the basic structure of the two phrases is the same). Both phrases denote groups whose identities are characterized by where they come 'from'. The implication is clear: 'those from works of the law' have lost sight of the sufficiency of faith, which is also to say they have lost sight of the fundamental character of the covenant established through Abraham. Whatever else they have done, they have failed to 'remain within' this fundamental part of 'all that has been written in the [first] book of the law [Genesis]'.

The other clue is given by the phrase 'works of the law' itself. For if our earlier exposition is on the correct lines, 'those who are from works of the law' were precisely those who saw obedience to the law in terms of the obligation to maintain Israel's distinctiveness as alone the people chosen by God for himself and thus separate from the (other) nations. Paul's point, then, in elaboration of his claim made in 3.6–9, is that

[32] E.g. H. Hübner, *Law in Paul's Thought* (Edinburgh: T. & T. Clark, 1984) pp. 18–19; H. Räisänen, *Paul and the Law* (WUNT 29; Tübingen: Mohr, 1983) pp. 94–5; Bruce, *Galatians* pp. 159–60; Longenecker, *Galatians* p. 118.

[33] See above pp. 76–7.

[34] For an earlier and fuller treatment, see my 'Works of the Law and the Curse of the Law (Gal. 3.10–14)', *Jesus, Paul and the Law* ch. 8. Cf. particularly G. Howard, *Paul: Crisis in Galatia* (SNTSMS 35; Cambridge University Press, 1979; 2nd edn 1990) ch. 3; T. L. Donaldson, 'The "Curse of the Law" and the Inclusion of the Gentiles: Galatians 3.13–14', *NTS* 32 (1986) pp. 94–112.

such a 'works of the law' attitude and praxis is in direct contrast to the gospel of justification by faith promised to the Gentiles. And once again, such a failure to appreciate and abide by the covenantal premise at the basis of the book of the law must mean failure to abide by all that has been written therein. One cannot claim to be faithful to the declared purpose of God while continuing to insist that Gentiles are excluded or can only be acceptable to God by becoming proselytes. Paul makes the point as sharply as he can: to continue to insist on works of the law is actually to breach the covenant on whose basis the law was given, and so to breach that law, entailing the curse of Deuteronomy.

It follows from this that the law and faith stand in sharp antithesis (3.11–12). It is an antithesis which the other missionaries would strongly resist (as Peter's conduct at the Antioch incident already demonstrated). But it is the immediate consequence of Paul's insistence on the sufficiency of faith, over against those who saw the law and obedience to it as much more fundamental to their identity as God's covenant people. The point is straightforward: the basis of acceptance by God (righteousness) is faith on the human side (Hab. 2.4). In contrast, the law has a different function: to indicate how life should be lived by the covenant people (Lev. 18.5). The two roles are quite distinct: it is not the function of the law to enable justification or to give life; that is the role of faith (3.11) and Spirit.[35] The law is not 'from faith', like justification; it is given to structure the life of the covenant people (3.12), but not in such a way as to undercut the basic character of that life as a living 'from faith' (3.11).

But what of the curse of the law under which Paul assigned 'those from works of the law' (3.10)? Paul's answer is that Christ bore this curse in his death and has thus liberated those who were under it (3.13). The text he cites, 'Cursed is everyone who has been hanged on a tree' (Deut. 21.23) did not originally refer, of course, to crucifixion. But we know from the DSS that such a link had already been made among the Qumran

[35] See below n. 47.

covenanters (1QpHab. 1.7–8; 11QT 64.6–13).[36] And it is quite likely that the same link was made in early polemic by other Jews, perhaps by Paul the persecutor himself, against Christian Jewish proclamation of a crucified Messiah. At all events, Paul here takes up the denunciation, and instead of refuting it makes it into a positive affirmation of the significance of Jesus' death on the cross.

The rationale begins to become clear when we set the verse properly in context. For the curse of the law is obviously the same curse as that spoken of in 3.10 (Paul modifies Deut. 21.23 to make the link clearer). That is to say, it falls on those who so live out of (the works of) the law as to keep Gentiles as such at a distance from the covenant people and thus also from the benefits of their covenant with God. Moreover, the purpose of Christ's bearing this curse of the law is explicitly 'that to the Gentiles the blessing of Abraham might come in Christ Jesus' (3.14). The situation where a curse lay upon those who kept Jew and Gentile apart so far as the blessing of Abraham was concerned has been brought to an end.

This suggests in turn that Paul understood the significance of the cross and its curse primarily in terms of its significance for the Gentile question – just as he understood both his own commissioning (1.15–16) and the gospel to Abraham (3.8) in the same terms. Probably (but this is more speculative) he had in mind that in Deuteronomy's terms to be accursed meant to be put out of the covenant people: the accursed one defiled the land of covenant promise (Deut. 21.23); the climax of the cursing of Deut. 27–8 was literally to be expelled from the land of promise (Deut. 28.63–8); and in 11QT the punishment of crucifixion was for those who were guilty of breaking the covenant bond.[37] In being himself crucified, therefore, Christ Jesus had been accursed by God, that is, had in effect been put outside the realm of covenant promise. And yet – this was the

---

[36] See particularly J. A. Fitzmyer, 'Crucifixion in Ancient Palestine, Qumran Literature and the New Testament', *CBQ* 40 (1978) pp. 473–513, reprinted in his *To Advance the Gospel* (New York: Crossroads, 1981) pp. 125–46.

[37] Cf. particularly F. F. Bruce, 'The Curse of the Law', *Paul and Paulinism*, C. K. Barrett Festschrift, ed. M. D. Hooker & S. G. Wilson (London: SPCK, 1982) p. 31; also *Galatians* p. 164.

discovery Paul made on the Damascus road – God had vindi-
cated and exalted this same Jesus. The corollary could not be
doubted: the God who had thus acknowledged Jesus the outsider had declared himself for those formally outside his covenant people. The God of Jesus was God for the Gentiles. Presumably this rationale was bound up with his immediate
conviction already noted (1.15–16) that this Jesus must be
preached among the Gentiles.

At all events, the conclusion Paul derives from this is one
which brings his argument back on to its central line – 'in order
that we might receive the promise of the Spirit through faith'
(3.14). Again the divine purpose is underscored, and again it is
the sufficiency of faith which is underlined. When Christ
removed the curse which lay upon the separated people of
God, he showed also the mistake of continuing to assume that
God's covenanted blessing was for Jews as distinct from Gentiles.[38] This double dismissal of the attitude and praxis of
'works of the law' allowed the original emphasis of the initial
promise to Abraham to re-emerge – as 'through faith' alone.
Implicit also is the conviction once again of the apocalyptic
significance of the cross – that what it brought about was the
eschatological fulfilment (the outpouring of the Spirit) of that
initial promise. The time promised to Abraham (3.8) was now.
In the new reality brought about by Christ the previously
divided Jew and Gentile had become the 'we' (both Jew and
Gentile) who have received the promised Spirit through faith.

THE ROLE OF THE LAW

Paul has thus far certainly made a strong case for affirming the
sufficiency of faith, and one which, with its appeal to their own
experience of faith, must have weighed heavily with his Galatians. But the longer he went on the more pressing became the
question not yet addressed: what then of the law? If faith was

---

[38] This is probably the key also to filling out 2.21: to insist that Christian Jews
continued to observe (the works of) the law as though nothing had changed was to
ignore the boundary-abolishing character of Jesus' death and to nullify the
restatement of the grace of God expressed therein.

the complete basis for the promised relationship with God
(2.19–20), if the law, despite being a means of ordering life
within the covenant people (3.12), had primarily served to
mark out and reinforce the distinctiveness of Jew from Gentile
and resulted in those of the works of the law being accursed,
then what was its function within the purpose of God? This
would be an especially urgent issue for those who remembered
that it was also said of Abraham that the promise of seed and
blessing to the nations was given to him 'because Abraham
obeyed my voice, and kept my charge, my commandments, my
statutes, and my laws' (Gen. 26.5).

Paul begins to address the question by underscoring the
primacy of the divine promise (3.15–18).[39] Divine promise is
the correlative of human faith; the covenant given to Abraham
by promise can only be fully received by faith. The actual line
of argument, however, is less than satisfactory. Given the
passage from Gen. 26.5 just cited, it was hardly enough to point
to the time gap between the promise being given to Abraham
and the giving of the law at Sinai (430 years; cf. Exod. 12.40).
And the thesis that a will could not be amended would hardly
carry much weight. More plausible was the claim that the seed
in view in the promise to Abraham of offspring was the Christ
(3.16), for the promise was first fulfilled in a single individual
(Isaac) and a passage like Ps. 89.3–4 could naturally suggest a
messianic interpretation.[40] But the main purpose of the paragraph was evidently to establish the character of the original
covenant with Abraham as one of promise, and to insist that
nothing since then had changed that basic character.[41] Otherwise Paul was simply clearing the ground for the principal
question, 'Why then the law?' (3.19).

The law and Israel

Paul's answer is in effect that the law had a temporary role as
guardian of Israel in the period prior to the coming of Christ

---

[39] The noun 'promise' is used eight times in 3.14–29, plus the verb in 3.19.
[40] See below pp.122–3.
[41] The perfect tense in 3.18 underscores the sense of gift once given and of continuing
validity.

and the eschatological fulfilment of the promise to Abraham. Somewhat surprisingly this is a rather controversial exposition, since most commentators regard the passage (3.19–4.11) as one of the most polemical against the law in all of Paul's writings. It is true, however, that the role Paul attributes to the law here has a negative side. So we will simply sketch out both emphases and attempt to reach a balance at the end.

According to 3.19 the law 'was added for the sake of transgressions'. This is usually understood in the light of the similar sounding passage in Rom. 5.20 – 'the law came in to increase the trespass'.[42] But 'for the sake of' could hardly be heard by the Galatians as 'in order to provoke'. On the contrary, Gal. 3.19 has a distinctly more positive ring to it, and probably should be taken more in the sense, 'in order to deal with transgressions'. In other words, Paul probably had in mind here the law's role within Israel to provide through its sacrificial system a means of atoning for transgression and thus of facilitating Israel's daily living within the covenant. In 3.19b the temporary nature of this role is made explicit – 'until there should come the seed to whom the promise had been given'. Similarly with Paul's talk of the law as 'having been ordered through angels' (3.19c). In face of the assumption of some that Paul here demonizes the law,[43] it needs to be recalled that the association of angels in the giving of the law was a quite familiar and unthreatening motif both in Jewish and elsewhere in Christian thought of the time.[44]

So too when Paul says, 'Before the coming of this faith we were held in custody under the law' (3.23). The principal verb was sometimes used in a negative sense ('hold in subjection'). But its principal sense was 'guard', 'watch over' (like a city garrison – 2 Cor. 11.32), 'protect', 'keep' (Phil. 4.7; 1 Pet. 1.5). So what Paul had in mind was almost certainly a protective custody – the law as a protection (as in 3.19a) against the

---

[42] E.g. Betz, *Galatians* pp. 165–7; Räisänen, *Law* pp. 144–5; Bruce, *Galatians* pp. 175–6, 180–1; S. Westerholm, *Israel's Law and the Church's Faith. Paul and his Recent Interpreters* (Grand Rapids: Eerdmans, 1988) pp. 178, 186.

[43] Particularly Hübner, *Law* pp. 24–36.

[44] Deut. 33.2 LXX; *Jub.* 1.29–2.1; Philo, *Som.* 1.143; Josephus, *Ant.* 15.36; *Apoc. Mos.* preface; Acts 7.38, 53; Heb. 2.2.

power of sin just referred to (3.22). The point is the same in the metaphor of the *paidagogos* in 3.24. The slave-custodian given charge of the young, to instruct in good manners, and discipline when necessary, was frequently remembered with mixed feelings – as still the case when adults today look back to tutors and teachers of their youth. More to the point here, however, is that the role of the *paidagogos* was essentially a positive one, and included the protection of the youth put in his charge.[45] As a transitory role – till the youth came of age – the metaphor fitted well the case Paul was building up.

At the same time Paul's argument does have more negative connotations for an understanding of the law's role. In 3.20 the most obvious meaning of a notoriously difficult verse[46] is that the role of Moses in mediating the law compares unfavourably with the immediacy of the promise given directly to Abraham by God himself. In other words, the law through Moses is not such a full expression of God's grace as the promise to Abraham. This is reinforced by 3.21: it was simply not the law's function to give life, 'to make alive'; that was the role of God directly through his Spirit.[47] Whereas, as already indicated by the quotation in 3.12, the role of the law was to regulate the life thus received, life lived within the covenant. To give the law a more fundamental role within Christianity (works of the law as indispensable to the life of faith), therefore, was to fall into a confusion of categories, to exalt the law, in effect, to the status of the Spirit.

More challenging is the fact that by linking the role of the law in relation to Israel so closely to the time before Christ, Paul was putting it effectively on the wrong side of the eschatological divide. The guardianship of the law ('under the law', 3.23, 25) was correlated with the rule of sin ('under sin', 3.22)

---

[45] See e.g. Longenecker, *Galatians* pp. 146–8.
[46] This is the verse of which J. B. Lightfoot, *Galatians* (London: Macmillan, 1865) made his much quoted comment, 'The number of interpretations of this passage is said to mount up to 250 or 300' (p. 146).
[47] 'To make alive' is a biblical term and is almost always a work exclusive to God (e.g. 2 Kings 5.7; Ps. 71.20; *Aristeas* 16; John 5.21; Rom. 4.17; 1 Cor. 15.22) or his Spirit, a particularly Christian emphasis (John 6.63; Rom. 8.11; 1 Cor. 15.45; 2 Cor. 3.6; 1 Pet. 3.18).

over the old age ('the present evil age' of 1.4).[48] Despite its ameliorating function, therefore (3.19a), the law could be said to have reinforced the rule of sin – Paul presumably still thinking of how reliance on the works of the law actually transgressed the fundamental character of the covenant (3.10).[49] Though even here Paul can see a virtue in these restrictive conditions of the time before Christ (3.22): that when the time of promise came to fulfilment (in the coming of Christ), the contrast with the preceding period of restriction would be a means of ensuring that the sufficiency of faith in Christ for the receiving of that promise would be clear.

A striking feature of Paul's theology thus emerges. Not just the role of the law as temporary guardian for Israel in the time before Christ, but the law in that role as analagous to that of a spiritual power (like sin). The effect was to diminish Israel's distinctiveness at a significant point. Typical of Israel's self-understanding was the assumption that God had appointed angels to direct other nations, but had chosen Israel for himself.[50] Now Paul in effect claims that the law functioned like Israel's guardian angel, and, by implication, put Israel in the same position as the other nations; the distinctiveness of the direct relation with God belonged to the promise to Abraham, not the law (3.15–20). Whether the role of the law as a kind of spiritual power/guardian angel is implicit in the contrast of 3.19–20 must remain hidden in the obscurity of 3.20. But it is certainly implicit in what Paul says in 4.3 and in the way Paul brings his argument to a climax in 4.8–10, where it is clear that for the Galatians to put themselves under the law was tantamount to reverting to their old pre-Christian enslavement to false gods, 'beings that by nature are no gods'.

Critically unclear is the point at which, in Paul's view, the divine purpose for the law merged into a criticism of his fellow

---

[48] This personification of sin as a power holding human existence in thrall is the only note in Galatians (apart from 2.17) of a theme which dominates the later treatment of Rom. 5.12–8.10.

[49] Here too Paul's treatment comes closer to the later argument of Rom. 7 than anywhere else in Galatians, though Rom. 7.14–25 echoes Gal. 5.17 clearly.

[50] Deut. 32.8–9; Sir. 17.17; *Jub.* 15.31–2; *1 Enoch* 20.5; *Targum Pseudo-Jonathan* on Gen. 11.7–8. On this paragraph cf. particularly Howard, *Crisis* ch. 4.

Jews for over-exalting the role of the law. The uncertainty will be due partly to the difficulty of apportioning responsibility (divine providence or human culpability) within a monotheistic framework. And partly, no doubt, to the considerable ambivalence Paul himself must have felt regarding the story of Israel in the light of the story of Christ – an ambivalence reflected in the positive/negative metaphors used by Paul in 3.19–25. At any rate, crucial for our assessment of Paul's theology at this point is the recognition that his more negative evaluation of the law was bound up with his reaction against the typical Jewish attitude to the Gentiles. That is to say, it was the law as epitomized in works of the law, and as seen to have its primary function in marking out Israel in distinction from the other nations, against which Paul polemicizes. For Gentiles to put themselves under the law understood in these terms was to revert to a regime under 'the weak and beggarly elemental forces' (4.9).

In all this, of course, Paul speaks from the vantage point of faith in Christ. From the perspective that Christ fulfilled the central promise of the covenant, the period of the law's guardianship of Israel could be regarded as temporary – until the coming of faith (3.23, 25). That this allowed a continuing role for the law disentangled from its role as Israel's guardian and correlated with faith is a theme to which we will have to return.[51] Here we must continue to trace out the most distinctive feature of his theology – his understanding of how Christians should relate to the story of Israel as now embodied in the Jews.

THE RELATION OF BELIEVERS TO ISRAEL

Integral to Paul's argument is that there is a direct linkage from the promise to Abraham to Christ as the promised seed, through whom the nations will enter the blessing of Abraham. In terms of the argument in Galatians, the link is from 3.8 through 3.16 to 3.26–9. This is how the story of Christ modifies

---

[51] See below pp. 114–18.

the story of Israel. The period of holding Jew and Greek apart in the era of the law's guardianship of Israel has been circumvented and left behind by the significance of Christ. Some of this would be recognizable to Paul's fellow Christian Jews on the basis of their common convictions. But Paul saw it as necessary to press home the point in a more thoroughgoing fashion.

Sonship and slavery

The section 3.26–4.11, 4.21–31 is dominated by the contrast between the status of son and slave ('son', 'heir' etc., 11 times; 'slave' etc., 9 times). Paul's point is simple: the faith which first received the covenant promise should now be directed to the one in whom that promise is fulfilled. Faith in Christ is now sufficient to ensure the relationship of all to God as sons (3.26), that relationship which hitherto had been the particular claim of Israel and of the righteous within Israel.[52] To be thus identified with Christ (3.27) also relativizes traditional distinctions of race, social status and gender (3.28), including, not least, that between Jew and Greek which was such a feature of the epoch of Israel under the law. And, more to the immediate point, faith in Christ, as commitment to Christ and belonging to Christ, ensured full participation in the heirs and heritage of Abraham (3.29). Paul builds here once again on the shared conviction and experience of faith and reinforces his argument for the sufficiency of faith.

Paul, however, goes on to liken this sonship to the maturity of the adult heir (4.1–7). The logic was straightforward, and in itself would have been in large part non-controversial to most Christian Jews. As previously noted,[53] the outpouring of the Spirit could be understood as the eschatological fulfilment of God's covenant promise to Abraham (3.14). Since all members of the new sect, Jews and Gentiles, had believed in Christ and

[52] Israel as God's sons, e.g. Deut. 14.1; Isa. 43.6; Hos. 1.10; *Pss. Sol.* 17.30. The righteous within Israel as God's sons, Sir. 4.10; 51.10; Wisd. Sol. 2.13–18; 5.5; 2 Macc. 7.34; *Pss. Sol.* 13.8.
[53] See above p. 61.

received the same Spirit, that proved that they were sons and heirs who had already entered into the fullness of their eschatological inheritance (4.6–7). The controversial feature begins to emerge with the corollary, that the status of Israel prior to Christ was like that of an heir under age (4.1–2). For it carried the implication that those who continued to cling to the law in its now outmoded role were in the same position. To be sure, this is the more positive way in which Paul describes the relation between his fellow Christians (Jew and Gentile) and his fellow Jews who continue to cling to the law in its guardian and divisive role. The latter are still heirs, still sons, albeit yet to enter into their full heritage.[54] And any eschatological hope was bound to relativize the period before fulfilment: Christ himself was 'born under the law' (4.4).

At the same time, however, Paul deliberately chose to develop a much more negative feature of that relationship. The heir under age was no better than a slave: to be under the guardianship of the law was like a form of slavery to the elemental forces of the world (4.1–3); to be 'under the law' was still to stand in need of liberation from slavery, still to lack that quality of sonship which is evidenced in the experience of the Spirit (4.5–6). If Jew and Gentile who have received the Spirit are no longer slaves but sons, the necessary corollary is that the Jew who has not yet believed in Christ is still in a slave-like condition under the law. This is why Paul was so astonished that his Galatian converts could want to revert to such a slave-like condition (4.8–9), where relationship with God was understood in terms of feast days rightly calculated (4.10),[55] rather than in terms of the immediacy of the experience of the Spirit (4.6–7).

Such a devaluation of their status could not but be offensive

---

[54] Note that Paul speaks of the child as 'lord of all' (4.1), presumably an echo and affirmation of the tradition which had grown up and which interpreted the inheritance promised to Abraham as the whole earth (Sir. 44.21; *Jub.* 17.3; 22.14; 32.19; *1 Enoch* 5.7; Philo, *Som.* 1.175; *Mos.* 1.155).

[55] A calendrical dispute about how to calculate the correct feast day (by the sun or the moon), which is reflected in *Jubilees*, *1 Enoch* and the DSS, shows how important such issues were within Judaism at that period; see my 'Echoes of Intra-Jewish Polemic'.

to the bulk of Paul's fellow Jews, and still today to the great mass of Jews who do not recognize Jesus as Messiah. It should be clear, however, that the theological rationale behind it has nothing to do with anti-Judaism, let alone anti-semitism; Paul speaks as a Jew of the significance of the life, death and resurrection of another Jew. The theology was much more eschatological in motivation, and carried as one of its primary features a protest against the ethnic divisiveness which Paul saw as a consequence of Jewish over-evaluation of the role of the law. Indeed, the only theological justification that can be given for Paul's theology at this point is that a realized eschatology of such existential power was bound to relativize whatever had come before. It was the theologically and experientially overwhelming character of the revelation of Christ and the experience of faith and the Spirit which cast all that Paul had previously held dear in the shadow. It is part of the character of such theology that it finds it hard to give ground to those who have not shared that experience. But for Paul at least, such experience was the living heart of the gospel and of the theology which the gospel entailed.

The two covenants

Paul's theology at this point receives its sharpest and most extraordinary expression in the allegory of Abraham's two sons (4.21–31). In it he sets out in opposing columns the antithesis he now saw between Christian Jew and Gentile on the one hand and non-Christian Jew on the other. The structure of the argument invites the expositor to set it out in table form:

Abraham had two sons (4.22)

one by a slave	and one by a free woman (4.22)
born according to the flesh	born through promise (4.23)

Allegorically the women correspond to two covenants (4.24)

Mount Sinai for slavery (4.24)	free (4.26)
= Hagar (4.24)	(= Sarah)
= the present Jerusalem (4.25)	= the Jerusalem above (4.26)
bearing children in slavery (4.25)	bearing children of promise (4.28)
according to the flesh (4.29)	born according to the Spirit (4.29)

The surprise comes in the amazing reversal of roles: that contemporary Jerusalem could be identified *not* with Isaac, from whom Jews had always traced their descent, but with Ishmael, the son of Hagar, who had been explicitly excluded from the line of promise through Isaac (Gen. 17.18–21) – an astonishing turnabout! The reasserted downgrading of non-Christian Jews to the status of slaves is simply the corollary of this extraordinary exegesis. Of course the perspective is once again apocalyptic and the antithesis eschatological in character. And Jews familiar with Jewish apocalyptic thinking would probably have been familiar with the eschatological antithesis between the present Jerusalem above,[56] with the similar implication that the present Jerusalem was an inadequate copy of the heavenly (cf. Exod. 25.9, 40). Even so, Paul's radical treatment of the theme must have been surprising, not to say offensive even to other Christian Jews, the other missionaries in particular.

The extremeness of the argument probably derives from the fact that Paul was responding to the other missionaries at this point. As several have argued,[57] it was probably the other missionaries who introduced the comparison of Abraham's two sons to the Galatians – to make the very different point, of course, that Abraham's inheritance came down to later generations through the line of Isaac, that is the children of Israel. Paul's allegory is therefore most likely intended as a response to the argument of the other missionaries. That is to say, the purpose was to remove it from the armoury of the other missionaries, not as a primary expression of his own theology; to disarm the other missionaries by demonstrating how the same episode in sacred scripture could be read in a way completely opposed to the other missionaries' gospel. That is why, presumably, it comes at the end of his main argument, as a kind of addendum to it, rather than as a principal part of his own argument; it was not intended as a plank in his own

---

[56] See above p. 51.
[57] C. K. Barrett, 'The Allegory of Abraham, Sarah and Hagar in the Argument of Galatians', *Essays on Paul* (London: SPCK, 1982) pp. 118–31, has been influential here. See also particularly Martyn, 'Law-Observant Mission'.

platform. Those who wish to be under the law on this issue should observe how easily the law can be heard to very different effect (4.21). Moreover, the fact that Paul uses the fundamental Jewish category of 'covenant' to describe *both* sides (4.24), where previously it seemed that he wanted to link promise with covenant (3.15–16) in distinction from law (3.17–18), indicates how little theological mileage he actually wanted to derive from the allegory. And presumably it is for similar rhetorical effect that Paul takes the final astonishing step of citing Gen. 21.10 against non-believing Jews: 'Throw out the slave girl and her son; for the son of the slave girl will never inherit with the son of the free woman' (4.30). The story of Abraham and his two sons, far from justifying the persuasions of the other missionaries, can be shown to justify their ejection from the church! If anyone is to be 'thrown out', it is those Jews who have lost sight of the character of the sonship covenanted to Abraham and who effectively deny it by putting more stress on their physical (Ishmael-like) descent from Abraham.

We should probably, therefore, discount to a fair degree the sharpness of the antithesis Paul poses in 4.21–31 between Christian Jews and Gentiles, as belonging to a quite different order from the rest of his fellow Jews. This is the language of polemic, an exegetical *tour de force*, a virtuoso performance, rather than sober theological argument. In fact, the allegory is simply an extreme expression of the same apocalyptic perspective which has underlain Paul's argument throughout. Once the eschatological significance of Christ has been recognized, and so also the apocalyptic transition between the story of Israel and the story of Christ, it follows that the status of Jews who have not accepted Jesus as Messiah was bound to be seen as less advantaged. We could hardly expect Paul to have been both transformed and energized by this revelation of Christ, and *not* to see his former life 'in Judaism' in a much dimmer light. We should also recall as a matter of some importance that Paul's argument at this point was not with Jews in general, but with Christian Jews – particularly the other missionaries who had presumably first introduced the theme of Abraham's two sons. It was an argument about how the new faith, which they both shared in one degree or other, should be seen to have affected their traditional Jewish faith. What the implications were for Jews who refused to accept Jesus as Messiah is a question which Paul addresses only later, in Rom. 9–11.

THE CONCLUSION – FREEDOM!

The word which Paul chooses to round off the main section of his argument is significant – freedom! It was the word he had chosen earlier to summarize the truth of the gospel as experienced by the Galatians (2.4–5). It was a theme which encapsulated the preceding exegesis (4.22–31) and the son/slave contrast which dominated the whole of chapter 4. But it was also no doubt a word drawn from the heart of Paul's own experience – that he experienced the essence of the gospel for himself as freedom. That is not to say that he had experienced his earlier life in Judaism as a form of slavery – not at all (1.13–14). Rather we should say that as he looked back on that life, that was how it *now* appeared, from the new eschatological perspective given him by the gospel. This should occasion no surprise: many who have grown out of a more conservative or fundamentalist expression of faith did not experience it as slavery – of course not. But as they now look back it appears to them as a form of slavery – in its over-defined character, its absorption in details, its failure to distinguish primary matters of faith from those now seen as secondary – a form of slavery from which they have been delivered. So it was with Paul: he saw not just the epoch under the law as a form of slavery (4.1–2), but his own encounter with the risen Christ as a liberation.

The freedom of which Paul speaks, in other words, is partly experiential – the liberty of the Spirit, the sense of a being set free for a closer relationship with God (4.5–6). And partly theological – the recognition that some things are more fundamental than others (the shared convictions, the sufficiency of faith), and that when priorities are properly perceived some of the beliefs that previously had been thought important need to be set aside or diminished in value precisely because they conflict with the primary beliefs. Many of those at such a stage in their own spirituality find it difficult to appreciate how things which are now so clear to them had been so hidden from them in the past and how it can be that they remain so hidden from others. Such was evidently Paul's own experience as reflected in the puzzled anguish and irritation of his abrupt cry here: 'For freedom Christ has set us free! Stand fast, therefore, and do not be subject again to the yoke of slavery!' (5.1).

In making this ardent and urgent plea Paul was seeking to press home the principal themes of his distinctive theology as argued for in the preceding chapters. To accept circumcision, as the other missionaries insist, would be to revert to slavery (5.1). It would involve adopting the whole Jewish way of life,[58] that is, reverting to the old epoch of life under the law (5.3). It would cut off from Christ because it would cut away the ground of grace (5.2, 4) and amount to a denial of their initiating experience of faith and grace (5.5). The apocalyptic transition has wholly relativized the old epoch's distinction between circumcision and uncircumcision and underscored the primacy and sufficiency of faith (5.6). The cross has nullified the old significance of circumcision as marking out those belonging to the people of grace and promise from those outside (5.11).

In sum, Paul shared with his fellow Christian Jews a warm appreciation of the eschatological significance of Christ and the cross, and of the importance of faith in Christ. But for Paul that significance focused in and came to its test case in a recognition that the heritage of Abraham was now fully open to the Gentiles, and on the same basis that it first was promised to Abraham – faith. The Galatians' own experience of faith and the Spirit was proof of that. Consequently the coming of Christ marked the end of the epoch when the focus of God's purpose was on Israel guarded by the law. The transition to the new age of fulfilled promise meant therefore that the old

---

[58] In other words, 5.3 probably implies the typical Jewish self-understanding that the Jewish way of life was a total package, with circumcision as the first step on a lifetime of observance, a complete way of life (see also below p. 103) – as in Lev. 18.5 (Gal. 3.12).

works of the law attitude and praxis, an expression of Israel's concern to maintain its distinctiveness as God's people from the other nations, was no longer appropriate. To continue so to live was to continue living in the old epoch and not yet in the age of the promise fulfilled in the gift of the Spirit. The continuity with Israel's story was still there, but in terms of the promise (to Abraham) fulfilled and the inheritance (of Abraham) entered into, and not in terms of the law.

Perhaps we should see the most concise summary of Paul's distinctive theology in his final blessing on the Israel of God (6.16). Presumably, understood in the light of his whole argument, that is the Israel of God's purpose, Israel defined by God's promise and Abraham's faith, an Israel where Jewish distinctiveness need no longer be maintained and in which Gentiles can be a part while still Gentiles. This redefinition of 'the Israel of God' is the most distinctive and still challenging feature of Paul's theology.

CHAPTER 5

How should the heirs of Abraham live?

The second principal theme of Paul's argument focuses on the issue, How then should we live? This was a natural and unavoidable question: in order to meet the challenges of everyday life one had to reflect on the practical outworking of one's social situation, religious obligation or philosophical principles. It was a question which absorbed the attention of many of the great minds of the age. At least since the time of Aristotle, ethics, the study of correct human action, had been a prominent topic for philosophers. Many of Paul's Galatian audiences would no doubt have been familiar, for example, with the Stoic conviction that the wise man lives in harmony with nature and with the social critique of wandering Cynic teachers. Listing of vices to be avoided and virtues to be cultivated (as in 5.19–23) was quite a common practice.[1] And household codes as in the later Paulines (Col. 3.18–4.1; Eph. 5.21–6.4) would probably also have been familiar. Equally important were the corollaries for individual conduct of the different social rituals which provided the framework for daily life within an ancient city – particularly some acknowledgement of the civic cult (mark of good citizenship), obligation to one's patron and participation in trade guilds or burial clubs – while some would find particular meaning in the rituals of a mystery cult.[2]

It was one of the features which seems to have proved most attractive about Judaism for many who would otherwise have

[1] See e.g. Longenecker, *Galatians*, pp. 249–52.
[2] For the larger picture see W. A. Meeks, *The Moral World of the First Christians* (Philadelphia: Westminster, 1986); A. J. Malherbe, *Moral Exhortation. A Greco-Roman Sourcebook* (Philadelphia: Westminster, 1986).

seen it simply as the ethnic religion of the Jews – their well-defined ethical codes and high moral standards. As Rom. 1.18–32 reminds us, Jews were particularly careful to distance themselves from Gentile idolatry and sexual ethos, emphases which evidently appealed to many proselytes and God-fearers. Josephus boasts more than once of how other nations sought to emulate the law of Moses, presumably with at least some justification, for example:

Our earliest imitators were the Greek philosophers, who, though ostensibly observing the laws of their own countries, yet in their conduct and philosophy were Moses' disciples ... advocating the simple life and friendly communion between man and man. But that is not all. The masses have long since shown a keen desire to adopt our religious observances; and there is not one city, Greek or barbarian, nor a single nation, to which our custom of abstaining from work on the seventh day has not spread, and where the fasts and the lighting of lamps and many of our prohibitions in the matter of food are not observed. (*Apion* 2.281–2)

And we should not forget how keenly wisdom was sought in the ancient world, not least the practical wisdom of everyday situations and relationships, and how prominent such wisdom is in the Jewish tradition, the wisdom of the Torah.[3]

We can well imagine, therefore, how important the issue was for the Galatians. By responding in faith to the message of Christ crucified, and by accepting baptism in the name of Jesus, they had made a decisive break with their old ways of life and committed themselves to something different. Like those who, according to Luke, had responded to Baptist's earlier call for repentance and baptism, they were bound to ask the question, 'What then shall we do?', seeking like them practical advice for everyday conduct (Luke 3.10–14). As now, so then, the conduct of everyday relationships and responsibilities would be the test of new faith, the proof of conversion.

And we can imagine too the effectiveness of the appeal made by the other missionaries: they had the answer – the Torah, the law of God. That was precisely why it had been given – to those

---

[3] E.g., Proverbs, *The Words of Ahiqar*, Wisdom of Jesus ben Sira, *Testaments of the Twelve Patriarchs, Pseudo-Phocylides*.

redeemed by God from the slavery of Egypt to show them how to live as his people. Like Abraham, having entered into the promise of faith, they should now keep God's commandments, statutes and laws (cf. Gen. 26.5). The logic was obvious and wholly biblical. It could also help explain why circumcision was being given such prominence by the other missionaries, despite the Jerusalem agreement (2.1–10). For circumcision could be presented not so much as the rite of entry to the covenant people ('getting in'), but as the first act of Torah piety for the new member of the covenant people (as it was for the newborn son of Jewish parents). This is the implication also of 5.3 – circumcision as the first action in a whole new way of life.[4] To Gentile converts who had repudiated their old ways of life, with its clear markers for social and individual conduct, and who had attached themselves to a strange social phenomenon, a religion without sanctuary, cult or priest, the appeal of such clear ethical and social guidelines must have been considerable.[5]

All this is reflected in one of the most consistent features in Galatians, its focus on what we might call 'the second phase'. It is most explicit in 3.3: what follows from the beginning they made? How do they think the completion of God's work in them will be accomplished? But the same concern lies behind almost every paragraph of the letter, in a whole sequence of variations. What follows from the gospel and its acceptance (1.6–7; 2.14)? What is the outworking of the grace of God (1.6)? For Paul it had been apostleship to the Gentiles (1.15; 2.9); for those he opposed it was evidently the law (2.21; 5.4). If the issue of circumcision for Gentiles was settled in Jerusalem (2.1–10), what of the issue of continuing life-style, as posed by the incident at Antioch over table-fellowship (2.11–14)? The other missionaries evidently gave the same answer as the group from James – 'works of the law': faith in Christ must be complemented and demonstrated by the observances laid down in the law

---

[4] See also above p. 99 n. 58.
[5] For a valuable exposition of Galatians as a response to such a challenge see J. Barclay, *Obeying the Truth. A Study of Paul's Ethics in Galatians* (Edinburgh: T. & T. Clark, 1988).

(2.15–16); this, after all, was the logic of 'covenantal nomism' – that the law shows how those already in the covenant should live within the covenant.[6] Paul's answer had thus far been to argue that the second phase marked by the law was not a model for individual Gentile conduct but a temporary phase in God's eschatological purposes for Israel (3.15–4.11). And that in the new epoch introduced by Christ, circumcision of Gentiles marked not the corollary to faith in Christ, but a decisive repudiation of that faith (5.1–12).

That, however, was his negative answer to the other missionaries. He was evidently concerned, and no doubt on his own part anyway felt it necessary, to give his own positive answer to the question still hanging over the whole crisis in Galatia: how then should we live? Paul's answer comes primarily in terms of the Spirit. If the first part of his own more distinctive theology (chapter 4) was an outworking of the convictions he shared more widely with fellow Christians, the second part (chapter 5) is an outworking of their shared experience.

BE LED BY THE SPIRIT

The initial clue is given by the passage already referred to, 3.3, Paul's indignant challenge to the Galatians: 'Are you so foolish? Having begun with the Spirit are you now made complete with the flesh?' It is particularly striking that Paul should thus give prominence to the Spirit in this the opening of his main argument to the Galatians. We have already pointed out that reception of the Spirit was a central feature of their shared experience, which would have been seen as confirming their status as members of the new movement, and which would have been the basis of their own confidence of having been accepted by God. It is equally clear that the gift of the Spirit was seen as the other side of the same coin from faith: the

---

[6] For 'covenantal nomism' see above p. 77 n. 24. In my earlier essay, 'The Theology of Galatians' (*Jesus, Paul and the Law* ch. 9), I put forward the thesis that 'Galatians is Paul's first sustained attempt to deal with the issue of covenantal nomism' (p. 242). At all events, the issue is best described in terms not of 'getting in' or 'staying in' (E. P. Sanders, *Paul, the Law, and the Jewish People* (Philadelphia: Fortress Press, 1983)), but of 'going on'.

one thing Paul wanted to know of them was whether they had received the Spirit by works of the law or by hearing with faith, whether God supplied the Spirit to them by works of the law or by hearing with faith (3.2, 5); the sufficiency of their faith was demonstrated by their manifest experience of the Spirit (so again 3.14).[7]

Now we must further note the clear implication that the Galatians' progress to 'completion' should be consistent with this beginning – that Christian completion should be as much 'by the Spirit' as their beginning.[8] This is the first clear note of what we have called the second principal theme of the letter. It was implicit in 1.6, where the implication is that the Galatians should have continued 'in the grace of Christ' by which they were originally called by God.[9] And it is implicit again in 5.5, 'we by the Spirit, from faith, are awaiting eagerly the hope of righteousness'. As the beginning, so the continuance – by the Spirit, through faith. However, it is only with 5.16 that the theme is addressed directly and in more detail.

A charismatic ethic

The importance of the Spirit as the key to responsible ethical conduct for the Christian is clearly indicated by the way Paul structures the main section of his exhortation (5.16–6.6). For it falls into two major paragraphs (5.16–24 and 5.25–6.6), both beginning with an exhortation to let conduct be determined by the Spirit: 'walk by the Spirit' (5.16); 'if we live by the Spirit, let us also follow the Spirit' (5.25). It is worth noting the terms

---

[7] See again p. 60 and n. 51.

[8] C. H. Cosgrove, *The Cross and the Spirit. A Study in the Argument and Theology of Galatians* (Mercer University Press, 1988) pp. 85–6 maintains that the issue on which the other missionaries appealed so effectively to the Galatians was how to maintain the supply of the Spirit. But there is no suggestion that Paul thought the Galatians' 'supply of the Spirit' was diminishing; the past tense of 3.3 ('having begun') is complemented by the present tense of 3.5 ('he who continues to supply the Spirit to you and continues to work miracles among you . . . '). Their experience of the Spirit is the presupposition rather than the goal of Paul's argument.

[9] God calling in grace (1.6) = God supplying the Spirit through faith (3.3); see above p. 59 n. 50.

in which Paul expresses these thematic exhortations, as also the language of 5.18, 'If you are led by the Spirit'.

In 5.16 the metaphor of 'walk' meaning 'conduct yourselves' is as typically Jewish as it is untypically Greek. Moreover, Paul would have been well aware that the typical Old Testament use of the metaphor called for God's people 'to walk in (God's) laws or commandments or statutes'.[10] Paul's language, therefore deliberately echoes the language by which the other missionaries would have made their appeal to the Galatians. Implicitly, then, Paul shows his own Jewishness: there is an appropriate life-style to be expected of the heirs of Abraham. But the strength of the echo also serves to bring out by way of contrast the distinctiveness of Paul's counsel: their walk is to be determined not by the law but primarily by the Spirit.

A similar contrast appears in 5.18: 'If you are led by the Spirit you are not under the law.' When used in connection with the Spirit, the verb 'led' implies the sense of being constrained by a compelling inner force, or of surrendering to a powerful inner compulsion (cf. particularly Luke 4.1; Rom. 8.14; 1 Cor. 12.2). Here, evidently, the understanding of the Spirit is of a power which works like a deep-rooted passion or overmastering compulsion. This experience is quite different from that of being 'under the law'. To be 'under the law' was to live a life determined by the written law and national traditions of the Jews, by external constraint of custom and rule (cf. 3.23–5; 4.1–2). To be under the Spirit is to know the freedom of external constraint replaced by internal desire and compulsion.

Another expression of 'the second phase' issue is 5.25, for it calls again for consistency between beginning and continuation, or between basic principle and its outworking. Since they owe their lives as believers to the Spirit, the new quality of life brought by the Spirit, the way they live their lives should display the same character. By implication Paul recalls the apocalyptic transition between the epoch of the law and that of

---

[10] E.g. Exod. 16.4; Lev. 18.4; 1 Kings 6.12; Jer. 44.23; Ezek. 5.6–7. The technical term for rulings on disputed issues of conduct within Judaism is Halakah, from the Hebrew *halakh* = 'to walk'.

the Spirit: their lives should reflect this. And again there is an implicit contrast with a definition of covenant life in terms of doing what the law commands (cf. 3.12): living is defined in terms of the Spirit, not in terms of the law's requirements. The verb translated 'follow' means basically 'to stand in line', and carries with it a sense of order imposed by an authority or in accord with a recognized standard. Paul takes it for granted, in other words, that the Spirit is not an anarchic power, disruptive of all order, but produces good order.

This repeated contrast between Spirit and law as the source of Paul's ethics nevertheless sets alarm bells ringing for many Christians. For the history of Christianity is littered with individuals and groups who, claiming direct inspiration from the Spirit of God, have thrown over inherited structures and traditions and claimed divine authority for new revelations and patterns of worship and life. Does Paul stand in that line, and his teaching here give support to such 'enthusiasm'? Does Paul anticipate and to that extent validate the wilder claims and excesses usually attributed to Montanists, the spiritual or radical reformers, or some Pentecostal evangelists?

In this potentially fractious issue what is needed above all is a sense of proportion and balance. Paul's emphasis on the Spirit here is consistent with his emphasis earlier in Galatians on the importance of the experience of the Spirit (3.2–5, 14; 4.6–7). He must therefore have been envisaging a life-style and choice of conduct options which constantly referred to that inner consciousness of the Spirit's presence and which sought to bring the life of the Spirit to expression in daily life. The repeated contrast with the law implies an inward rather than an outward point of reference in matters of ethical decision. This is presumably what Paul had in mind when he spoke elsewhere of discerning God's will by means of a renewed mind, of being given discernment to approve what was best in any particular situation (Rom. 12.1–2; Phil. 1.9–10). Paul was claiming in effect that the inner, spontaneous knowledge of God's will, for which Jeremiah had looked as a feature of the new covenant (Jer. 31.31–4), was now a reality in the experience of those who had received the Spirit. In other words, the

Spirit brought about the inward reality of a circumcised heart and a more immediate communion between God and believers (cf. Rom. 2.28–9; Phil. 3.3).

The remainder of the chapter constitutes a progressive clarification of this issue – of what it meant for Paul in practical terms to be 'led by the Spirit'. In the first place we should note another indication of the character of the Spirit-led life in what it produces – antagonism to the 'flesh' and the 'fruit of the Spirit'.

Flesh and Spirit

The antithesis between flesh and Spirit is a repeated theme in Galatians: having begun with the Spirit the Galatians should not think to be made complete with the flesh (3.3); they stand in sharp antitheses as those 'born in accordance with the Spirit' over against those 'born in accordance with the flesh' (4.29); they are warned that 'those who sow to their own flesh shall from the flesh reap corruption, but those who sow to the Spirit shall from the Spirit reap eternal life' (6.8). But the contrast is dominant in the section 5.16–25:

I tell you, walk by the Spirit and you will not satisfy the desire of the flesh. For the flesh desires against the Spirit, and the Spirit desires against the flesh; for these are opposed to one another, to prevent you from doing those things you want to do. But if you are led by the Spirit, you are not under the law. And the works of the flesh are plain ... But the fruit of the Spirit is ... And those who belong to Christ Jesus have crucified the flesh with its passions and desires. But if we live by the Spirit, let us also follow the Spirit.

Here Paul immediately shows his awareness of the dangers of cutting loose from all constraints and traditions. The opening words of his exhortation underline the same point: 'You were called to freedom, brothers; only not the freedom for opportunity to the flesh' (5.13). By 'flesh' Paul obviously means the merely human appetites and desires – the sort of 'works of the flesh' which he goes on to list in 5.19–21, beginning with 'unlawful sexual intercourse, impurity, debauchery', and ending with 'envyings, drunkenness [and] excessive feasting'.

It was well appreciated in philosophic discussion regarding freedom that there were two kinds of slavery – the slavery of the individual to a human master, and the slavery of the soul to vice and passion; to be truly free, one had to be free also from the domination of the passions.[11] Paul agreed. Reception of the Spirit could not be an excuse to kick over the traces and do whatever one wanted. On the contrary, it was precisely the function of the Spirit to oppose such self-centred indulgence. In this way too Paul indicates that being led by the Spirit will be in accord with the initial reception of the Spirit: for it was precisely faith's open trust in God to which the Spirit was given (3.2); and such openness to God is quite the reverse of the selfish indulgence of merely human desires.

Indeed, in one of the most striking verses Paul ever wrote (5.17), Paul describes the Christian condition as one of permanent inward contradiction, the experience of constantly being pulled in opposite directions. According to Paul it is a simple fact of spiritual experience that what the Spirit and the flesh desire are mutually contradictory: the flesh craving for satisfaction of its mortal needs, ever tending to see self-gratification as sufficient end in itself; the Spirit, by implied contrast, desiring a fuller life, looking beyond the satisfaction of the merely human desires to a higher level of relationship of the human creature with its Creator (cf. 4.6–7) and with other humans as equally God's creatures (cf. 5.22–3). Also clearly implied is that this condition will last for believers so long as they continue in the flesh (cf. 2.20).

Most striking of all is the sharpness of the conflict envisaged by Paul and the way he pictures the believer as caught on both sides of the inward struggle: the flesh desiring against the Spirit and the Spirit desiring against the flesh 'are opposed to one another to prevent you from doing those things you want to do' (5.17).[12] According to Paul, believers should not be surprised to find themselves, in part at least, and not just sometimes, unwilling and antagonistic towards the leading of the Spirit; that is simply themselves as flesh 'desiring against the Spirit'.

[11] I am almost quoting from Philo, *Prob.* 17 here.
[12] On 5.17 see particularly Burton, *Galatians*, pp. 301–2.

But they should also expect to experience desires in themselves which oppose and prevent them doing just what their fleshy appetites urge on them. Evidently for Paul this inward struggle would be a continuing feature for believers, since it is in fact the expression of the Spirit's invasion of the human sphere and lasts as long as the human condition lasts (cf. Rom. 7.14–25).[13] This is why, presumably, following the Spirit (5.25) is no mere passive act of 'being led by the Spirit' (5.18), but requires also a resolute intention to 'walk by the Spirit' (5.16); the balance between passive and active will be deliberate. In the same way, Paul seems to balance talk of being crucified with Christ (passive, 2.19 and 6.14) with the talk of believers having 'crucified the flesh with its passions' (5.24); but we will return to that point.

One other feature of the flesh/Spirit antithesis calls for comment. It is the fact that Paul uses the term 'flesh' also to characterize the attitude and objectives of the other missionaries: their policy for the Galatians would have the latter trying to achieve completion 'with the flesh' (3.3); they represent an 'according to the flesh' sonship of Abraham (4.29); 'they are trying to compel you [the Galatians] to be circumcised' in order 'to make a fair showing in the flesh' and 'in order that they might boast in your flesh' (6.12–13). Obviously the thought was most immediately prompted by the fact that circumcision is a cutting of the flesh ('my covenant in your flesh', Gen. 17.13). But Paul evidently saw the fleshly character of circumcision as characterizing also the attitude and objectives of the other missionaries: they were putting too high a value on the flesh. On the one hand that meant prizing too highly their physical descent from Abraham (over against those not so descended from Abraham). On the other hand it meant boasting in the accession of proselytes to Judaism as further proof of Israel's distinctiveness before God.[14]

[13] See my *Jesus and the Spirit* pp. 308–18.
[14] As in Paul's treatment of 'boasting' in the most closely parallel context of Rom. 2.17, 23 and 3.27, what is in view is most probably a Jewish boasting in Israel's standing before God and within the law, that is, boasting in ethnic identity and privilege over against the (other) nations.

The point is that Paul does not seem to see any difference between that fleshly attitude and the attitude condemned in 5.19–21: such policies as those pursued by the other missionaries were also 'works of the flesh' (probably a play on 'works of the law', 5.19); the bulk of the list of these works ('hostile actions, strife, jealousy, displays of anger, selfish ambitions, dissensions, factions, envyings', 5.20–1) were probably intended to characterize the situation in Galatia brought about by the 'agitators';[15] hence also the implication of 5.18–19 that 'under the law' and 'works of the flesh' go together. This was the other main thrust of Paul's response to the other missionaries: to come (again) under the law is *not* the way of countering the flesh, rather it is a way of pandering to it; Israel's pride in ethnic identity as the chosen people is itself a work of the flesh. As Paul was to argue more fully in Rom. 7–8, the answer to the flesh is not the law (particularly Rom. 7.18, 25; 8.3) but the Spirit (particularly Rom. 8.2–4, 12–14).

The fruit of the Spirit

The antithesis to the works of the law is the fruit of the Spirit (5.22–3). 'Fruit' was a natural and well-known metaphor to indicate the consequences or results of conduct, whether good or evil.[16] Here, however, Paul speaks of the fruit of the Spirit – that which is produced in the first place not by human activity but by the indwelling power of God. The contrast between 'works' and 'fruit' also recalls the opening antitheses of 3.2–3, with, once again, the implication that that which the Spirit produces will be an expression of the same open trust in God with which the Galatians began. And the different contents of the two lists likewise suggest a contrast between activity and character. Where the one list breathes an air of anxious self-assertiveness and frenetic self-indulgence, the other speaks more of concern for others, serenity, resilience and reliability.

---

[15] The point is often recognized; see e.g. Barclay, *Obeying* 153–4 and n. 31; Cosgrove, *Cross* p. 157.

[16] F. Hauck, *karpos, TDNT* 3.614; in biblical usage see e.g. Prov. 1.31; Jer. 17.10; Matt. 3.8 par.; John 15.2–8.

The first list is all about human manipulation of others for selfish ends, the second all about the divine enabling and engracing which brings about a transformation from inside out, from character to conduct.

It is no accident of composition that love stands at the head of the list, for that is the most distinctively Christian element in the list,[17] and it may be that Paul intended that the rest of the list should be seen as expressions of the one all-embracing Christian grace of love.[18] Because of its importance we shall need to give 'love' separate and fuller attention below. But here we should note that, in common with all the rest of the fruit, what is in view is a character trait, not simply loving actions – love as the primary expression of the Spirit in its opposition to the works of self-indulgence and self-gratification, love as a deeply felt concern for others, an inward compulsion which turns the individual outward in service of others. The implication is that without that inward transformation from inside out, Christian conduct even in the name of love can quickly degenerate into works of the flesh (cf. 1 Cor. 13.1–3).

Other elements in the fruit of the Spirit have also a strong experiential or emotional dimension, particularly the next two, joy and peace. It should be noted, however, that Paul would not have thought of either of these in individualistic terms: 'joy' was characteristically for Paul a shared experience strengthening bonds of community (e.g. Rom. 15.32; 2 Cor. 8.2; Phil. 2.29–30; Philemon 7); and in Jewish thought 'peace' was not reducible to a personal tranquillity but included all that makes for social well-being and harmonious relationships.[19]

The rest of the list consists in virtues more widely recognized. Who could deny the positive qualities of 'patience, kindness, goodness ... gentleness, self-control'? It is worth noting that Paul does not hesitate to appeal to such characteristics as would generally be lauded by all fair-minded people; Christian

---

17 Unlike the others in the list of virtues, 'love' was a little used word at that time. Christians, however, took it over and made it their own (the noun occurs 116 times in the NT, 75 of them in the Pauline letters).

18 So e.g. V. P. Furnish, *Theology and Ethics in Paul* (Nashville: Abingdon, 1968) p. 88; Longenecker, *Galatians* p. 260.

19 See further W. Foerster & G. von Rad, *eirene*, *TDNT* 2.400–20.

character must meet the test of the best standards of human virtue. Though again it should be noted that Paul attributes these no less than love to the Spirit; the same openness to the Spirit that marked the beginning of their Christian experience (3.2) and continuance of their relation with God (4.6) is the source of the fairest human qualities that marked their human relationships. And once again a contrast is implicit with the factiousness of the 'works of the flesh' as illustrated in the activities of the other missionaries.

The other element in the list worth special mention is 'faith'. It was also a commonly recognized virtue, in the sense 'good faith, trustworthiness'. But in a letter where the association between Spirit and faith, in the sense of open trust in and commitment to the one proclaimed in the gospel, is so important (3.2, 5, 14; 5.5), it is likely that Paul made no marked distinction between the two meanings. The faith which is unconditional trust in God alone, as expressed in the Galatians' first receiving of the gospel, finds outward expression in love (5.6) and in the good faith and trustworthiness which were more widely applauded.

Paul's claim, then, is a bold one: that the character traits which all people of good will desire for themselves and their community, as summed up in the highest Christian 'virtue' of love, are the result of the action of the divine Spirit working within individuals. This will also be why he was so hostile to the other missionaries: to insist on visible rituals and ethnic markers like circumcision and special days (4.10) was to forget that patterns of living must be inspired from within rather than imposed from without; without the inner spontaneity and immediate directness of the Spirit in the human heart, the policy of the other missionaries was a recipe for a renewed form of slavery. At the same time, such an emphasis on the Spirit cannot be dismissed as an enthusiastic ethic or arbitrary situation-ethic. For what Paul had in mind was clearly transformation of character more than individual actions. Indeed, we might say that in the second list he avoided recommendation of specific conduct, for the conduct he sought to encourage is charismatic in that it is the fruit of inner transformed character rather than conduct determined solely by rule book or tradition.

Most interesting of all is the suggestion that in drawing up his list of Spirit-fruit Paul had in mind a kind of character sketch of Christ, that the character of Christ as attested in the Gospel tradition provided the pattern and yardstick for Christian character. The suggestion can hardly be proved in relation to the list itself, but it gains credibility in the light of the second main strand of Paul's ethical teaching, as we shall now see.

CHRIST AS THE PATTERN

The other side of Paul's ethic is the place he gives to what we might call the external norm – the *inward* compulsion of the Spirit expressed in accordance with and measured by the *outward* norm of Christ.[20] It does not receive the same explicit emphasis as the leading of the Spirit, because in Galatians any emphasis on external norm could be seen as giving ground to the other missionaries. It was because they gave so much emphasis to the external norm of the Torah that Paul, partly by way of reaction, gave such prominence to his more charismatically determined ethic. Nevertheless, Paul's ethic does work with an external norm. That much was implicit in the extent to which he accepted such a widely recognized list of virtues as evidence of the Spirit's working (5.22–3). But its most distinctive feature is summed up in what Paul calls 'the law of Christ' and love of neighbour.

The law of Christ

Paul had already given clear indication of the importance of love as the mark of Christian conduct: 'In Christ Jesus neither circumcision counts for anything, nor uncircumcision, but faith operating effectively through love' (5.6). It was not simply the sufficiency of faith alone which made works of the law irrelevant; it was faith expressed in loving action which

---

[20] Many years ago my thinking on this subject was influenced by R. N. Longenecker, *Paul, Apostle of Liberty* (New York: Harper & Row, 1964) ch. 8.

wholly relativized the distinction between circumcision and uncircumcision, between Jew and Gentile. Where such love was manifested who could deny that this was a fruit of the Spirit, a mark of God's acceptance, a proof that God did not require works of the law as a *sine qua non* of faith's commitment? As Paul could assume the symbiotic relation of faith and Spirit (3.2, 5, 14; 5.5), so now he assumes a similar integration of faith and love. The whole of Paul's ethic, in fact, revolves around these three words – faith, Spirit, love. Faith and Spirit marked the going on, as well as the beginning of life as a Christian for Paul, not least because he was confident that such immediate trust in God and reliance on his Spirit could not find expression in other than love. Love of neighbour is the other side of the coin of love of God.

It is not surprising, then, that even before his principal emphasis on walking by the Spirit, Paul gives first place in his ethical exhortation to a call for love – 5.13–14: 'For you were called to freedom, brothers; only not the freedom for opportunity to the flesh, but through love serve one another. For the whole law is fulfilled in one word, in the well-known, "You shall love your neighbour as yourself"' (Lev. 19.18). What would probably strike his first readers most immediately is that Paul here appeals to the law. After warning his Galatian audiences so emphatically against any assumption that the law lays down rules which continue to be binding on all the heirs of Abraham, Paul's own first explicit ethical exhortation is drawn from the law! Moreover, other Jewish teachers were willing to sum up the whole law in a single command or principle, if not so often in terms of Lev. 19.18 as such, certainly in similar terms.[21]

What are we to make of this? Was Paul not being simply inconsistent and self-contradictory? Some have so con-

[21] Lev. 19.18 is not made much of in Jewish literature before Paul. But Paul's older contemporary, Hillel, is recalled as summarizing 'the whole law' in the negative form of the golden rule (*b. Sabb.* 31a); according to both Mark 12.32–3 and Luke 10.26–8 a scribe also summed up the law in terms of the two great commands calling for love of God and love of neighbour; and early in the second century rabbi Akiba is said to have described Lev. 19.18 as 'the greatest principle in the Torah' (*Gen. Rab.* 24.7).

cluded.[22] Others have attempted to resolve the quandary by distinguishing 'doing the whole law' in 5.3 from 'fulfilling the whole law' in 5.14, on the grounds that Paul could not have had any desire to encourage any sort of performance of the law.[23] The answer, however, lies more probably in recognizing the role which Paul had sketched out for the law in chapter 3 – that is, as peculiarly related to Israel in the period before the coming of Christ. With the transition to a new epoch, the law's role as guardian of Israel's distinctiveness was at an end. The obligation to walk in a way appropriate to the relationship given by God remained. But that was now more fittingly expressed in terms of the faith, Spirit and love which welled from the heart. Whereas the practices which served primarily to maintain Israel's set-apartness from Gentiles were wholly relativized and could now be seen to be of no consequence.

Paul was thus engaged in the delicate art of trying to have his cake and eat it, that is, trying to retain some emphases of the law while dispensing with others. The fact that his teaching on this point has caused such confusion among subsequent commentators is indication enough that he was not altogether successful. Without attempting further clarification, to achieve which we would have to press on into Romans, it will have to suffice here to note that despite his more dismissive language of 3.15–5.12 Paul did continue to maintain an external norm for Christian conduct, and that he summed it up in the love command drawn from the Torah. It was not only the promise to and heritage of Abraham that marked the firm line of continuity with the story of Israel, but also Torah focusing the obligation of human relationships in the command to love the neighbour.

Almost certainly a factor of decisive significance for Paul was the tradition that Jesus himself had so summed up the obligation of the Torah in respect to inter-human relationships

---

[22] Particularly Räisänen, *Law*, p. 62–73.
[23] Cf. Hübner, *Law* pp. 36–40; Westerholm, *Law* p. 203. The two phrases translated 'the whole law' are different, but synonymous (in the Matt. 22.39–40 parallel to 5.14 the 5.3 phrase is used). The verb in 5.14 probably has the sense 'brought to full expression, shown to have its complete meaning' (BAGD, *pleroma* 3).

(Mark 12.31 pars.). For the stimulus to focus on Lev. 19.18 in particular as a summation of the law was more distinctively Christian than Jewish, and it makes most sense of the data to attribute that stimulus to the memory of Jesus' own teaching, as the Gospel tradition implies.[24] In which case the further implication is that Paul would see Jesus' own ministry as showing what love of neighbour meant in practice, as illustrated both in his parable of the good Samaritan (Luke 10.29–37), in his own openness to sinners and Gentiles (e.g. Mark 2.16–17; Matt. 8.5–13; cf. Gal. 2.14–15),[25] and not least in his death on the cross (2.20). No better model for a self-giving sacrificial love which reached out to embrace the marginalized and outcast could Paul ask for.

All this suggests that Paul was familiar with the character of the Gospel traditions of Jesus' life and teaching. The fact that he does not attribute such teaching explicitly to Christ suggests further that such traditions would be familiar among the Galatian churches, so that the allusions would be recognized. Paul could certainly have been expected to pass on such foundation traditions to his new churches (cf. e.g. 1 Thess. 4.1; 2 Thess. 2.15; 3.6). Such allusions to them as 5.14, like the allusions to shared formulations such as those in 1.1 and 4, or to key Old Testament texts as in 2.16, confirmed the shared discourse of their faith precisely because chapter and verse were unnecessary.[26]

It is probably this shared knowledge of the Jesus tradition to which Paul refers in 6.2 when he sums up his exhortation in the words 'Bear one another's burdens and thus you shall fulfil the law of Christ'.[27] Certainly the cluster of echoes of Jesus' teach-

---

[24] Explicit reference to Lev. 19.18 is lacking in Jewish literature before Paul, but Lev. 19.18 is the Pentateuchal passage most often cited in the earliest Christian literature (Mark 12.31 pars.; 12.33; Matt. 5.43; 19.19; Rom. 13.9; James 2.8; Did. 1.2).

[25] See above pp. 74–5.

[26] The usual assumption that Paul could only draw on Jesus tradition by explicit quotation and attribution is unrealistic. Ch. 3 above gave only some indication of the range of common tradition Paul presumably could take for granted. One of the measures of the quality of community is the degree to which communication can proceed simply by allusion to shared knowledge and intimacies. Cf. particularly R. B. Hays, *Echoes of Scripture in the Letters of Paul* (New Haven: Yale University Press, 1989).

[27] See also e.g. Barclay, *Obeying* pp. 126–35; Longenecker, *Galatians* pp. 275–6.

ing in these paragraphs, on serving others (5.13), on love of neighbour (5.14), on the kingdom of God (5.21) and on cruci- fying the self (5.24), build up to a strong inference that familiar Jesus tradition was in Paul's mind when he dictated these words.[28] That is to say, 'the law of Christ' is probably Paul's summary for the traditions which documented the way Jesus lived, taught and died. He did expect the Galatians to fulfil the law, but it was the law as summed up in the love command and as illustrated and prioritized in Jesus' own ministry. It is in this way that the story of Jesus transforms the story of Israel and Israel's law.[29]

Transformed to Christ

Recognition of the importance of the story of Christ for Paul brings to light one further strand in Paul's ethics which might otherwise have laid hidden from view. For it is not a major theme of Galatians, at least in the sense that it is not high- lighted and developed. But it is referred to so frequently that it must be regarded as a major plank in his theology, and it may indeed be part of the foundations of Paul's ethics, which would also help explain its half-hidden character.

A term which catches the essence of this motif in Galatians is 'transformation'. To be transformed into angelic splendour was one of the ways of characterizing Jewish hope at this time, particularly in apocalyptic thought.[30] And transformation into a god-like being was the great goal for the initiate in mystery cults, as classically illustrated by the account of the initiations of Lucius into the Isis cult in Apuleius, *Metamorphoses* 11.23– 30.[31] Paul in effect agrees that something as radical as personal transformation is essential if the enervating power of the flesh's weakness is to be successfully countered. But for him the template and goal of Christian transformation is Christ.

---

[28] Note the parallel with Rom. 13.8–10, 14.17–18 and 15.1–3. On 5.21 see above p. 50 n. 41.

[29] See also R. B. Hays, 'Christology and Ethics in Galatians: The Law of Christ', *CBQ* 49 (1987) pp. 268–90.

[30] E.g. Dan. 12.3; Sir. 45.2; Mark 12.25; *2 Enoch* 22.8(A); *2 Bar.* 51.3, 10–12.

[31] See further particularly Segal, *Paul the Convert* ch. 2.

This is implicit in the easily overlooked (because so familiar) phrase 'in Christ', which occurs no less than seven times in Galatians (1.22; 2.4, 17; 3.14, 26, 28; 5.6). It was as 'in Christ' that the Galatians were free, sharing in Jesus' own freedom with respect to the law (2.4). It was as 'in Christ' that they could be called sons of God, bonded together as one family in the heritage of Abraham (3.14, 26, 28), sharing in his own sonship of Abraham. It was their being 'in Christ' which relativized the old distinction between Jew and Gentile (5.6), because Christ himself in his ministry and particularly in his death had abolished the curse which divided covenant member from outsider (3.13).

That this involves somehow a becoming like Christ is more clearly expressed in four other verses. (1) 2.20 – 'It is no longer I that lives, but Christ lives in me.' The old 'I' has died and been replaced by a new focus of personality, Christ himself. The 'I' which found social identity 'in Judaism' now finds personal meaning and identity in Christ and those who are also 'in Christ'. (2) 3.27 – 'As many of you as were baptized into Christ have put on Christ', where both metaphors indicate a transformation of personal status, a being put 'into Christ' and a taking on the character of Christor.[32] (3) 4.6–7 – 'In that you are sons, God sent the Spirit of his Son into our hearts, crying "Abba! Father!" Consequently you are no longer a slave, but a son.' The Spirit can now be recognized as the Spirit of Christ, who effects in the believer the same relationship of sonship with God.[33] (4) 4.19 – 'My children, over whom I am again in the pain of childbirth until Christ is formed in you.' The metaphor

---

[32] Putting on new clothes was widely seen as an image of taking on new characteristics or of spiritual renewal (see e.g. Isa. 61.10; Zech. 3.3–5; see further A. Oepke, *enduo*, *TDNT* 2.319). In the theatre, to 'put on' someone meant to become that person for the purposes of the play (BAGD, *enduo* 2b). See below p. 131.

[33] Gal. 4.6–7 together with Rom. 8.15–17 demonstrate (1) that the *abba* prayer was widely characteristic of the new movement, (2) that the Spirit inspiring it was recognized to be the Spirit of Jesus, and (3) that it was understood to attest a share in Jesus' sonship and inheritance. This implies that the *abba* prayer was seen by the first Christians as a *distinctive* prayer form, linking them with Jesus and inherited from him (cf. Luke 11.2), and so confirms the indications of the Gospels that the *abba* prayer had been distinctive of Jesus' own spirituality. See further my *Jesus and the Spirit* ch. 2; also *Christology* pp. 26–33; Scott, *Adoption* pp. 182–5.

is strained but its meaning clear: the objective of Paul's missionary and pastoral exertions is that the Galatians display more and more the character of Christ. In all three texts the unspoken assumption is that the risen Christ is the image of God, that is, the pattern of what God intended for humankind.[34] In the terms of simple piety, the objective for believers going on in the Christian life is that they become like Jesus.

Most striking of all, however, is the way Paul focuses the challenge of this becoming like Christ once again in the cross. In talking of his own death to the law and new life Paul inserts the phrase, 'I have been crucified with Christ' (2.19). The tense in Greek is perfect, not aorist. That is to say, the meaning is not, I was once crucified with Christ, an event over and done in the past; but, I was at that time nailed to the cross with Christ, and continue in that state, still hanging on the cross. The believer's on-going experience is one of dying with Christ. Presumably it will be only when the flesh with its desires has decayed completely away, when the mortal body has been transformed into the spiritual body of the resurrection, that the process of sharing in Christ's death will be ended (Cf. Rom. 8.11–23). The tense is the same in 6.14: the mutual crucifixion of the world to me and of me to the world is a permanent state of this human existence for the believer.[35] The crucifixion of the flesh with its passions and desires which marked their coming to belong to Christ (5.24) should not be thought of as completed in a single act. Conformity to Christ (4.19) is a lifelong process.

Here again, then, Paul sees the cross at the heart of the story of Jesus. The cross not only marks the transition from old world to new creation (1.4; 6.14–15), not only stands absolutely opposed to anything which limits the grace of God or persists in setting division between peoples (2.21; 3.13–14), but also sets the pattern for Christian conduct as self-giving love (2.20). In this way not least the ethic of the Spirit is conformed to the pattern of the cross; the Spirit whose lead the Galatians must follow is the Spirit of the crucified.

---

[34] This is explicit elsewhere in Paul; note particularly Rom. 8.29; 1 Cor. 15.45–9; 2 Cor. 3.18–4.4; Phil. 3.10–11, 21; Col. 3.10.

[35] On 6.17 see above p. 32 n. 19.

CHAPTER 6

Lesser issues

To complete our study of the theology of Galatians we should note briefly other elements which Paul himself only touches on, or which we have had to pass over too briefly in the more schematized analysis of the last two chapters.

PAUL'S USE OF THE OLD TESTAMENT

Paul cites the scriptures (the sacred writings of Judaism were the only scriptures they had) explicitly at a number of key points in his main argument:

3.6	Gen. 15.6	3.13	Deut. 27.26, 21.23
3.8	Gen. 12.3, 18.18	3.16	Gen. 13.15, 15.18, 17.8, 24.7
3.10	Deut. 27.26	4.27	Isa. 54.1
3.11	Hab. 2.4	4.30	Gen. 21.10
3.12	Lev. 18.5	5.14	Lev. 19.18

That all but two of them come from the Pentateuch, the Torah, is a further reminder of the importance Paul placed on demonstrating the continuity between the story of Israel and that of Christ. In addition, there is clear dependency on scripture at numerous other points – 2.6 (e.g. Deut. 10.17; 2 Chron. 19.7), 2.13 ('the church of God'), 2.16 (Ps. 143.2), 3.17 (Exod. 12.40), 3.19 (Deut. 33.2) and so on. It is easy to see, then, how much the terms and themes of scripture shaped Paul's own thought, no doubt often subconsciously. Scripture was his native air, the text-book of his education, the language of his own theology.

His use of scripture in Galatians, however, contains two

passages of particular note, for they both strike the modern reader as contrived and unconvincing – 3.16 and 4.21–31. They thus raise the question as to how valid was Paul's use of scripture, and whether he treated it simply as a wax nose, to be shaped to his own ends. We have already dealt briefly with the two passages in chapter 4, but a few more words under this heading are in order.

The first is 3.16, Paul's interpretation of the promise to Abraham and his seed (Gen. 13.15, 17 LXX; 15.18; 17.8; 24.7): 'But the promises were spoken to Abraham and to his "seed". It does not say, and to his "seeds", as to many, but as to one – "and to your seed" – who is Christ.' One problem is that the promises referred to had the land of Canaan in view – 'To your seed I give this land.' How could Paul refer promise of land for Abraham's offspring to God's acceptance of Gentiles? The answer probably is that it was already quite common to understand the promise of territory in a more symbolical way. Already before Paul the promised land was seen as symbolizing a more universal realm.[1] And in *2 Bar* 14.13 and 51.3 it is taken as a symbol of the world to come. Just as earthly Jerusalem could be seen as the shadow of a heavenly Jerusalem (4.26), so the promised land could be seen as symbolizing the hoped for blessings of the age to come, otherwise expressed in the outpouring of the Spirit. And since the original promises were combined with promise of blessing to the nations (3.8) Paul's treatment would have been quite acceptable.

Potentially more controversial is the argument based on the fact that 'seed' is a singular noun. For, of course, it is a collective singular: the promise was for 'seed' as numberless as the dust of the earth or the stars of heaven (Gen. 13.16; 15.5.)! And Paul himself was well aware of this, as his own argument later shows (3.29; cf. Rom. 4.16, 18). However, the very fact that Paul could so argue elsewhere confirms that he was not attempting to pull wool over anyone's eyes in 3.16. The point is rather that 'seed' is an ambiguous word, and Paul felt free to play on that ambiguity without manipulation or deceit. After

---

[1] See above p. 94 n. 54.

all, as already noted, the initial promise had a single individual in view (Isaac), and the same ambiguity is present in the promise to David of seed (2 Sam. 7.12; Ps. 89.3–4). Indeed, precisely the match between promise to Abraham's seed and to David's seed would probably have been enough to suggest the appropriateness of a messianic interpretation of the former as well as of the latter. Such an interpretation was thoroughly Jewish in character and occurred to more Jewish teachers than Paul.[2]

The interpretation of Genesis involved, therefore, was wholly appropriate in its own terms and time and provided a neat solution to the riddle of how to relate promise of blessings to nations with promise of land to Abraham's descendants. Those to whom these promises are now merely a curiosity of history will no doubt regard Paul's interpretation of them in the same light. But for those who regard these promises as still in some way definitive for Jewish and Christian self-understanding, the plausibility of Paul's interpretation will presumably continue to carry some weight.

The second passage, 4.21–31, is of interest because Paul explicitly describes his interpretation as 'allegorical' (4.24) – the word occurring only here in biblical Greek, but quite frequently in the Jewish philosopher, Philo, and in the Christian Fathers. The basic assumption of allegorical exposition is that the text has a deeper meaning or reference than appears on the surface. The danger of such exposition is obvious – that the deeper meaning is arbitrarily imported into and read out from the text, a meaning, in other words, determined not at all by the text but solely by a dogmatic or social world view imposed on the text. Such abuse of allegorizing resulted in the widespread condemnation of the practice in modern times and has given the term a somewhat pejorative overtone in much twentieth-century theology.

What of Paul's use of the term here in Galatians? Some, conscious of the pejorative character of the term, prefer to read 4.21–31 as an example rather of typological exegesis; that is, the historical details as given in the Genesis account were being

---

[2] See particularly M. Wilcox, 'The Promise of the "Seed" in the New Testament and the Targumim', *JSNT* 5 (1979), pp. 2–20; Bruce, *Galatians*, pp. 172–3.

treated as a typical expression of divine working and as fore-shadowing the eschatological fact of the gentile mission.[3] It is difficult, however, to deny a degree of arbitrariness in the exposition, particularly in the allegorical identification of Hagar (Abraham's slave-girl) with Mount Sinai (4.24), the interpretative move which enables Paul to turn the tables on the other missionaries.[4] On the other hand, the whole exposition has a logic consistent with the basic contrasts of the original story. Hagar's giving birth to Ishmael was a classic example of (Abraham's) failure to trust entirely on the divine promise alone; and Paul had already shown how ethnic Israel 'under the law' (of Sinai) could be likened to a form of slavery on other grounds. And from Paul's perspective the link between Isaac, as child of promise, and the promised Spirit, having now been received by Gentile believers, was a compelling one, a valid intermeshing of current and past experience of divine grace linked by divine promise.

On the whole, however, as already suggested, it is best to see 4.21–31 as a virtuoso performance by Paul, something of an afterthought to demonstrate how even the contrast between Isaac and Ishmael need not be counted in favour of the other missionaries' message. As such, it serves to illustrate a theology rooted elsewhere in scripture and experience, rather than as primary justification of that theology. As such, it is an example of how innovatively scripture can be used in such illustration. But it hardly provides justification for more arbitrary allegorizations, especially if offered as substantive argument for a theological assertion.

ECCLESIOLOGICAL ISSUES

We have already noted that by speaking of 'the church of God' in 1.13 Paul indicates his understanding of the church as in

---

[3] See e.g. A. T. Hanson, *Studies in Paul's Technique and Theology* (London: SPCK, 1974) pp. 94–5; Hansen, *Abraham* pp. 209–15. Paul's treatment of Abraham in 3.6–9 can also be regarded as typological; and Scott, *Adoption* ch. 3, argues that 4.1–7 contains a typological comparison between the first Exodus (from slavery in Egypt, 4.1–2) and the second Exodus of eschatological redemption (4.3–7).

[4] See above pp. 95–8.

direct line of continuity with the people of Israel met in assembly.[5] Here we need to correlate that observation with the fact that Paul also speaks of 'churches' in the plural – 'the churches of Galatia' (1.2), 'the churches of Judea' (1.22). For this stands in contrast to the regular Old Testament usage, which is almost always singular. Paul's language, of course, reflects the fact that the word had wider currency, denoting the gathering of a political body, or sometimes the business meeting of a club.[6] The point here, however, is that, despite the Old Testament precedent, Paul evidently did not think in terms of a single 'church'. Wherever and whenever Jews and Gentiles gathered 'in Christ' (1.22), they were 'the church of God'. The identity of these gatherings as 'church' evidently depended for Paul not on an organizational link-up or structure, but was given by their shared embrace of the gospel and experience of the Spirit, by their common incorporation into 'the Israel of God'. At this stage it was evidently more important for Paul to affirm the 'church'-ness of each individual gathering of believers in Judea and Galatia than to affirm that all these churches together formed one church.

The point is vividly illustrated by Paul's continuing attitude to the mother church in Jerusalem. We have already discussed briefly the tension evident in Gal. 1–2 in Paul's relationship with the Jerusalem leadership, and the breach with Jerusalem consequent upon Paul's presumed failure to withstand Peter successfully in the Antioch incident.[7] Here we need to note the continuing evidence of that breach in the way Paul speaks of the Jerusalem leadership in Gal. 1–2. The most striking indication is the phrase he uses repeatedly to describe them – 'those held in repute' (2.2, 6, 9). The phrase means literally, 'those who are influential, recognized as being something, who have a reputation'.[8] Paul thus acknowledges the high standing in which James, Cephas and John were held, but does so in a way which leaves it unclear whether he himself shared that view –

---

[5] See above p. 38 and n. 6.
[6] LSJ, *ekklesia*.
[7] See above respectively pp. 23–5 and pp. 13–14.
[8] BAGD, *dokeo* 2b.

those who are held in esteem (by others). The phrase thus has the character of a distancing formula – an acknowledgment of authority which includes a note of questioning.

Still more striking is the parenthesis Paul adds in 2.6 – 'what they once were makes no difference to me; God shows no partiality'. The dismissive note could hardly be clearer. The authority and reputation of the Jerusalem leadership might be firmly enough rooted in history – presumably in their historic association with Jesus himself, or in the initial establishment of the church in Jerusalem. And the present tense ('makes no difference') suggests that Paul himself had previously shared that high regard for the three Jerusalem leaders.[9] But now, at the time of writing, presumably in the wake of the fiasco at Antioch and the resulting breach with Jerusalem, Paul dismisses that authority with a disillusioned shrug: so far as the truth of the gospel was concerned, the reputation of the Jerusalem leadership no longer counted as of particular significance, and could certainly not outweigh the Galatians' own experience of divine acceptance; 'God shows no partiality.'[10]

This says something of interest about Paul's ecclesiology. Just as he wanted to maintain continuity with the church of God and the Israel of God, while also holding firm to the conviction that he had been called to take the gospel to the nations, and just as he maintained a positive tension between the tradition he initially received in converting to the way of Jesus and the immediacy of the initiating revelation of Jesus itself, so here he attempted to maintain recognition of the authority of the Jerusalem apostles (2.2) while insisting that his own interpretation of their shared convictions was essential if the truth of the gospel was to be preserved. At the end of the day ecclesiastical authority, as indeed his own apostolic authority,[11] was to be subservient and subordinate to the gospel, since the gospel of cross and Spirit was itself the source and measure of that authority.

[9] See again pp. 24–5.
[10] Note again also the downgrading of 'present Jerusalem' in the allegory of 4.21–31 (above p. 96).
[11] See above p. 25.

As for the leadership of the churches established by Paul, we should note that his letter is probably best read as a vigorous attempt to counter attempts made from Antioch or Jerusalem to undermine his own role and authority as church founder and to assert the authority of Antioch or Jerusalem over the Galatian churches. The letter itself, therefore, constitutes a rebuttal of a centralized authority seeking to impose a uniform church- and life-style on all churches. This is why the historic and enscripturated Paul is always liable to be seen as a threat to such authority. A gospel which can be both 'for the uncircumcision' and for the 'circumcision' (2.7) contains and requires a greater diversity than most institutional authorities can ever be wholly comfortable with.

The theological tensions which thus break surface in Galatians have considerable potential consequences for a fully rounded and biblically informed ecclesiology. But as the issues are somewhat tangential to the theory of Galatians itself, and since an adequate discussion of them would be bound to focus much more on Paul's theology of 'the body of Christ' as expounded elsewhere in his letters, we should not pursue them further here.[12] Suffice it to say that if Galatians counts for anything at this point it is to underline the importance of maintaining a vital tension between charismatic initiative and the constraints of tradition.[13]

Two other verses illuminate two other facets of Paul's conception of Christian ministry. The first is 6.1: 'Brothers, if a person is detected in some transgression, let you who are spiritual restore that person in a spirit of gentleness, keeping an eye on yourself lest you also be tempted.' The verse is somewhat obscure, including the question of who it is Paul here appeals to as 'you who are spiritual'. A particular (leadership) group, already recognized as such, is possibly in view. But he

---

[12] This applies also to 3.28, of which all that can be said here on the issue of ministry is that it must be judged very unlikely that Paul would have allowed gender or social status as such, any more than race, to constitute a barrier against any service of the gospel; see further E. S. Fiorenza, *In Memory of Her. A Feminist Theological Reconstruction of Christian Origins* (London: SCM, 1983), ch. 6.

[13] In recent years cf. particularly H. Küng, *The Church* (London: Burns & Oates, 1968).

nowhere else appeals to such a group to give a lead over the
more fractious issues treated earlier; and it is less likely that
Paul would give encouragement to the suggestion that only
some within the Galatian churches were 'spiritual', with the
implication that the rest were not so. More likely Paul was
issuing a general appeal to his readers, who had all, after all,
received the same Spirit (3.2–5, 14; 4.6), in the hope that some
at least would be sufficiently in tune with the Spirit to know
how to handle the delicate situation envisaged (cf. I Cor. 6.5).
That is to say, he probably saw pastoral leadership as also
charismatic in character – that as the larger group sought the
leading of the Spirit (5.18) some would be enabled to deal with
the case in question, thus demonstrating the character of their
spirituality, but with an authority to be recognized by all those
acknowledging the Spirit's direction (cf. 1 Cor. 14.37;
16.15–18; Phil. 3.15).[14] The general exhortation to 'bear one
another's (6.2) and reminder of personal responsibility ('each
will have to bear his own load', 6.5) confirms the same general
impression.

   The other passage of relevance is 6.6: 'let the one who is
taught share in all good things with the one who teaches'. The
principle that those who taught something of value should be
supported by followers or sympathisers was familiar in the
ancient world, and Paul elsewhere affirms that financial
support from Christian communities was essential if the ministry of the gospel was to flourish (Rom. 15.24; Phil. 1.5; 4.15).
Here, interestingly it is the ministry of teaching which is in
view. Presumably those themselves well informed on the distinctive Christian traditions (about Jesus) and interpretations
of scripture were expected to serve the church by instructing
new members in what the new faith was all about. The direction that they should receive support implies that there was
already a substantial amount of Christian tradition to learn
and to teach, and that to fulfil the ministry adequately would
take so much time as to prevent the teacher earning his own
living wholly by other means.

[14] See further my *Jesus and the Spirit* pp. 287–8; Barclay, *Obeying* p. 157.

At all events, it is striking that the first 'professional' ministry mentioned in the New Testament is teaching, since it confirms the importance of the word (the gospel) and of instruction in Christian tradition from the beginning.

Baptism

Given the importance that the Christian sacraments were to assume in subsequent centuries it is perhaps surprising that there is so little said in Galatians on this score. The lack of mention of the Lord's Supper in the Antioch incident (2.11–14) is particularly striking. It has to be assumed that Peter's eating together with the Gentiles (2.12) at least included meals which began with the broken bread and ended with the shared cup 'in remembrance' of Christ (cf. 1 Cor. 11.23–5). And it is natural to assume that the pain of Peter's separation from the Gentile believers was the pain of having to eat the bread and wine 'in remembrance' of Christ separately. But to put it thus may reflect more of modern ecumenical sensitivities than of the historical situation. The fact is that Paul gives no hint of this aspect of the affair. And the impression is strong that it was the abuse of table-fellowship itself – table-fellowship such as had marked Jesus' own ministry with 'sinners' – which caused Paul such indignation. At all events, the meal table as focus of fellowship in the early churches is clearly assumed by Paul.

Commentators have regularly found more references to baptism, not just in 3.27, but also in various other allusions. Heinrich Schlier, in particular, finds allusions in 2.16, 19–20, 3.2–4, 4.6–7 and 5.13, 24, as well as in both halves of 3.27.[15] This is questionable exegesis. Most would agree that we have to assume that all the first Christians were baptized, since the fact of baptism in the name of Christ always seems to be taken for granted as the act of initiation in the New Testament. And Paul presumably had baptized some at least of the Galatians personally, though 1 Cor. 1.14–17 warns us against any

---

[15] H. Schlier, *Galater* (KEK; Göttingen: Vandenhoeck, 1965) 4th edn, index 'Taufe'.

deduction that Paul counted his performance of baptism as an essential part of his ministry of the gospel. But that simply makes it all the more surprising that he does not make more explicit reference to these baptisms.

In contrast, as we noted in chapter 3, Paul gives repeated reference back to the Galatians' reception of the Spirit. This was evidently experienced in such a tangible way that participants like Paul were in as little doubt as to the Spirit's incoming to the lives of the Galatians as the Galatians were themselves (3.2–5; 4.6). Which also signifies that the experience of the Spirit must have been the focal point of the Galatians' conversion and adherence to the new faith proclaimed in Paul's gospel. It is that to which Paul recalled them directly, not as a hidden deduction drawn from their visible baptism. It is particularly noticeable that in seeking to counter the appeal which the other missionaries made to the need for circumcision Paul nowhere responds by setting baptism against circumcision. Nowhere does he say in effect, 'You do not need the rite of circumcision, because you have already received the rite of baptism; you do not need circumcision because you already have its eschatological equivalent in baptism.' The contrast of 3.2–3 is between an act of Torah obedience like circumcision (reinforcing fleshly and ethnic characteristics) and the immediacy of their reception of the Spirit through hearing with faith. The eschatological fulfilment of the covenant promise (sealed in circumcision in the flesh) is the Spirit sealed in the heart (3.14; 4.6–7; cf. Rom. 2.28–9; 2 Cor. 1.22; Phil. 3.3). We may doubt, moreover, whether Paul would have thought to suggest that baptism had replaced circumcision, lest baptism be given the same exclusive force as his opponents gave circumcision.[16] At any rate, there can be no doubt, from Galatians at least, that for Paul faith and Spirit were the primary factors in entering into the heritage of Abraham and sonship to God, and in fact the only factors which needed to be stressed let alone mentioned when the chips were down.

The one exception seems to be 3.26–7 – 'You are all sons of

---

[16] Cf. Burton, *Galatians* p. 205; Betz, *Galatians* pp. 187–8. See further my *Baptism in the Holy Spirit* (London: SCM/Philadelphia: Westminster, 1970).

God, through this faith, in Christ Jesus.[17] For as many of you as were baptized into Christ have put on Christ.' Here there is a general consensus that 3.27 is a reference to Christian baptism as such, though baptism presumably as an expression of the more regularly emphasized faith (3.26). However, that too should probably be questioned more than is usually the case. That the rite of baptism provided a particularly vivid metaphor (as did circumcision) had been recognized since the metaphorical use was first coined by John the Baptist (Mark 1.8 pars). And Christian tradition recalls both Jesus (Mark 10.38–9 pars.) and the first Christians (Acts 1.5; 11.16) taking up and adapting that metaphorical use for their own purposes. The most obvious inference from 1 Cor. 12.13 ('we were all baptized in one Spirit') is that Paul in turn had taken up the original Baptist's metaphor and (as in Acts) applied it to the experience of the Spirit poured out in the heart (Rom. 5.5; 1 Cor. 12.13c).

In which case it is an attractive deduction that in Gal. 3.27 Paul draws on a double metaphor (as also in 1 Cor. 12.13) to describe the way in which the acceptance of trusting faith and the gift of the Spirit accomplished the identification of the believer with Christ on which Paul's whole argument hangs (3.29). What the experience of faith and the Spirit were accomplishing was the beginning of that personal transformation indicated in such verses as 2.20 and 4.19, transformation into the image of God embodied in Christ.[18] Another way of describing that was by using the metaphors of baptism and of putting on clothes – to be immersed into Christ, to put on the character of Christ. That Paul can also use the latter metaphor elsewhere of the repeated and continuing responsibility of the believer (Rom. 13.14; cf. Col. 3.10–12; Eph. 4.24) is a further reminder that what is in view is an on-going process, as, again, in Gal. 2.19 and 4.19.

---

[17] The two phrases, 'through faith' and 'in Christ', describe the two sides of the divine-human relationship for the Galatian Christians – given status within the heritage of Abraham by being 'in Christ', a status received by them 'through faith'. The two should not be taken as a single phrase ('through faith in [*en*] Christ'), a construction which appears only in the deutero-Pauline letters; see my '*Pistis Christou*' p. 734 n. 25.

[18] See above pp. 118–20.

At the same time it is an equally obvious inference that baptism could provide such a powerful metaphor because the experience of being baptized in water was itself so powerful. Presumably the rite itself and the experience of the Spirit were often part of a single experience – hence the vitality of the metaphor, and the force of subsequent theology of the sacrament (a physical act with spiritual significance). Nevertheless, if we are to take the theology of Galatians seriously, both Paul's appeal to the Galatians and his theology of the gospel's effectiveness find their focus and rationale in the sufficiency of faith in the crucified and the experience of the Spirit.

CHAPTER 7

The influence of Galatians in Christian thought

There are two periods in which Paul's letter to the Galatians has been particularly influential – the early Church, including the New Testament period itself, and the modern period, from the Reformation onwards.

THE EARLY CHURCH

The New Testament period

We have already indicated the strong likelihood that Galatians was one of Paul's earliest letters, one in which he laid out his claim to full apostolic authority for his gospel and his under-standing of justification by faith, perhaps for the first time in just these terms, but certainly for the first time in a definitive writing, so far as we know. Within the Pauline corpus, there-fore, Galatians has a primary place as the first extant statement of Paul's distinctive theology. We cannot, of course, speak of the influence of Galatians on the rest of Paul's letters – the living Paul was himself the link! But because of its raw, spon-taneous character Galatians can be regarded as the closest thing we have to 'pure paulinism', and so serve as a pole of comparison by which to measure the subsequent course of Paul's theology.

On the whole the impression is of a fire which flared up on the news from Galatia, but which thereafter burned with a steadier flame. Attempts to interfere in his work by other 'apostles' or to impose circumcision on his converts continued to touch a raw nerve and to provoke new outbursts of passionate indignation (2 Cor. 10–13; Phil. 3). But otherwise issues over which Paul fought tenaciously in Galatians could be simply assumed. In the Corinthian correspondence, for example, the focus of Paul's attention had shifted to other matters. So themes over which he had sweated blood in Galatians are taken more or less for granted, not least justification and God's righteousness (1 Cor. 1.30; 6.11; 2 Cor. 5.21) and the role of the law (1 Cor. 7.19; 9.20; 15.56). And even the fact that some did not regard him as an apostle could be mentioned simply in passing (1 Cor. 9.2). And in Romans the significance of the cross is drawn on simply by making use of formulaic statements (Rom. 3.24–5; 4.24–5; 8.34).

In other cases it may be necessary to speak of Paul having second thoughts or revising the argument of Galatians. In particular, the theme of Gal. 3 is closely parallel to that of Rom. 4. But in the latter Paul avoids the weak argument that the time-lag between the promise to Abraham and the giving of the law proves that the law constitutes no qualification of the promise. Instead, his equivalent argument is based on the fact that Abraham had been pronounced righteous prior to and without reference to his being circumcised and on a careful exposition of the character of Abraham's believing. He also avoids the sharp antithesis between the two covenants represented by Hagar and Sarah used in Gal. 4.21–31, although in 2 Cor. 3 he proffers an equally sharp antithesis between the old and new covenants represented by Moses and Christ on the different theme of ministry. The strains which the story of Christ imposed upon the story of Israel, unexplored in Galatians (cf. 6.16), also provide the main thrust in the climax of Romans (9–11).

On two other points in particular it has been claimed that Galatians maintains a more extreme position from which Paul felt it necessary to withdraw. One is with regard to the law. Hans Hübner in particular finds it necessary to 'assume that there was a far from trivial theological development on the part of Paul between the two letters' on this issue.[1] He has in mind

---

[1] Hübner, *Law* p. 55.

the much sharper critique of circumcision as such in Galatians (contrast Rom. 2.25 and 4.11), and what he regards as the very negative treatment of the law in Gal. 3.19 and 21 (contrast Rom. 3.31 and 7.7–12). It is true that Paul, somewhat surprisingly, does not repeat the argument on the temporary role of the law so prominent in Gal. 3.15–4.11. But his more sophisticated analysis of the role of the law in Rom. 7 is actually of equivalent weight in claiming in effect that in the epoch 'under sin' the law is experienced as an enslaving power; and the effect of the argument in Rom. 2.25–9 is to relativize circumcision as much as Gal. 5.6. Moreover, we have already seen reason to question whether Gal. 3.19 and 21 should be interpreted in such negative terms as Hübner maintains; and the inability of his thesis to cope adequately with Gal. 5.14 undermines the whole contrast. On the whole then it is better to see Paul's discussion of the law in the two letters as different in content and in tone, but the same in theological intent.

The other is the thesis of John Drane[2] that Paul's treatment in Galatians gave several hostages to Gnostic thought – in basing the authority of his gospel on 'revelation', in devaluation of the law (Gal. 3.19 again), and in the liberty of the Spirit as a principal motif in ethics. Such emphases, he suggests, are strikingly similar to those which subsequently characterized Paul's opponents in Corinth. From which it may be deduced that these opponents learned these emphases from Paul himself, perhaps even quoting his own statements in Galatians to prove their own point of view.[3] 1 Corinthians, in its reaction against this teaching, would therefore constitute a withdrawal from the more exposed charismatic theology of Galatians,[4] while Romans could be regarded as the synthesis of the theses and antithesis of Galatians and 1 Corinthians. The overall thesis is attractive in its simplified neatness, but the attempt to detect such develop-

---

[2] J. Drane, *Paul Libertine or Legalist?* (London: SPCK, 1975).
[3] The Corinthian teaching was 'Paul's gospel overdone' (Drane, *Paul* p. 100). Cf. J. C. Hurd, *The Origin of 1 Corinthians* (London: SPCK, 1965).
[4] 'In 1 Corinthians ... he [Paul] tries to define in a quasi-legalistic fashion the ways in which the Spirit ought to do this (conform to Christ), and therefore in effect he limits not only the exercise but also the substance of the liberty which he had earlier expounded in Galatians' (Drane, *Paul* p. 71).

ment between the four main Pauline letters is as questionable in Drane's case as it is in Hübner's. So, for example, the weight being put on the heavenly disclosure of the Damascus road so far as Paul's gospel was concerned is as great in 2 Cor. 4.4–6 as it is in Gal. 1.11–16. And if Paul had been scared away from talk of being led by the Spirit (Gal. 5.18) by the enthusiasm for spirits in Corinth (1 Cor. 12.2; 14.12), it is odd that he should define 'sons of God' so uninhibitedly as 'those who are led by the Spirit' in Rom. 8.14. In this case too, it would seem, differences in emphasis and detail, determined in large part at least by the different situations being addressed, are being blown up into matters of substance.

It is more plausible, however, to see evidence of some strains between Paul's account of things in Galatians, and other first-century Christian leaders as represented by other writings in the New Testament. Not that we have any testimony from the other missionaries of Galatia, or indeed from Paul's opponents, even though Galatians itself makes clear that those who disagreed in at least some measure with Paul's interpretation of the gospel as expressed at Antioch and in Galatians included the other two most prominent leaders of earliest Christianity – Peter and James. But, as is well known, the letter attributed to James hints at disagreement on 'works of the law' and on how to interpret Gen. 15.6 and the significance of Abraham's faith (James 2.20–4). And though 1 Peter is usually thought to reflect Pauline influence (e.g. 1 Pet. 4.10–11), those more explicitly claiming to represent Pauline tradition (the Pastorals), who might be thought to be the heirs and proponents of Paul's distinctive theology, seem to have retained key features only as a traditional emphasis and in diluted fashion. So, for example, with regard to justification (Tit. 3.5–7), while the role of the Spirit seems to be much more ecclesiastically determined (1 Tim. 4.14; 2 Tim. 1.6).

Moreover, Olof Linton has made the interesting suggestion that some of the traditions repudiated by Paul in Galatians recur in Acts.[5] For example, that Paul went directly from

[5] O. Linton, 'The Third Aspect. A Neglected Point of View. A Study of Gal. 1–2 and Acts 9 and 15', *Studia Theologica* 3 (1949) pp. 79–95.

Damascus to Jerusalem (Acts 9.23–6), and that he did accept an additional obligation (the 'apostolic decree') at the Jerusalem consultation (Acts 16.4). We might add the fact that Luke seems willing to allow Paul the title 'apostle' only in the lesser sense of 'missionary' commissioned by the church at Antioch (Acts 13.1–3; 14.4, 14; contrast 1.21–6). The point is that in Acts Luke seems to retain accounts and assessments of Paul against which Paul himself protests most vigorously (Gal. 1.1, 11–12, 17; 2.6). Acts, therefore, probably reflects the fact that the degree of isolation which Paul experienced after the Antioch incident and expressed in Galatians probably continued, and that versions of events which Paul had attempted to rebut in Galatians still carried influence in many other churches. Galatians, in other words, represents Paul and Pauline theology out on a limb, and although that limb grew larger and stronger until it dominated the trunk, in its first-century setting Galatians still retains something of that initial 'out on a limb' character.

The patristic period

The significance of Galatians as a theological resource continued well beyond the New Testament. Indeed, as the spectrum of Christianity steadily lengthened, Galatians itself was one of the major focal points of debate between different factions and viewpoints. Not surprisingly, the letter which catches most clearly the sense of a new faith opening up to challenge a wider world continued to be a source of inspiration for more radical efforts in the same direction and an aggravation to those of a more conservative temperament.

The most striking illustration of the former is Marcion who successfully established a radical form of Christianity in the 160s and 170s in which Christianity's heritage of the Old Testament and from Judaism was totally disowned.[6] For Marcion Paul was the only legitimate apostle; all the rest had diluted and distorted the true teaching of Jesus because of their

---

[6] For a recent brief account of Marcion see *ABD* 4.514–16.

kinship with Judaism. Paul it was who set gospel and law in antithesis, and by resisting so forcefully the representatives of the religion of the Old Testament had demonstrated the essential character of Christianity. And Galatians was the primary testimony to this, and was therefore set by him at the head of the Pauline collection of letters to serve as the window through which all the rest should be read. Thus 1.1 and 11–12 could be read as a denial of any dependence of the gospel on the Judaism of the Jerusalem leadership, 1.8 as a dismissal of the gospel taught by the lesser god (angel from heaven) of the Jews, 2.11–14 as Paul once again refusing to allow the gospel to be determined by influence from Jerusalem, and 4.21–31 as necessitating the rejection of the Jewish religion *in toto*.

In a similar way, Gnostics, representing the other main radicalization of second-century Christianity, saw Paul as 'the apostle' – 'the apostle of the heretics', was Tertullian's riposte.[7] And for them too Galatians was fertile ground. So they could appeal to Paul's own legitimation through direct revelation, could read the allegory of Gal. 4 as contrasting psychic sonship with pneumatic sonship, and could take Paul's stress on the liberty of the Spirit (Gal. 5) and exhortation to the pneumatics in 6.1 as addressed to them.[8] That Galatians was retained within the canon of the great Church despite such use and abuse by Marcion and the Gnostics attests not only the fact that its association with the great apostle was irrefutable but also its inherent power as a prime expression of the Christian gospel.

At the other end of the spectrum come those continuing Christian Jewish groups represented in the pseudo-Clementines. These include sections which are generally regarded as directed against Paul, as the one most responsible for the rest of Christianity's rejection of the law. And once again it is Galatians which focuses the concern and the polemic. The most widely recognized refutation of Paul comes in the *pseudo-Clementine Homilies* 17.13–19 where Paul under the guise of

---

[7] See e.g. the brief treatment in my *Unity and Diversity in the New Testament* (London: SCM, 1977, 1990) 2nd edn, pp. 288–91.

[8] E. Pagels, *The Gnostic Paul* (Philadelphia: Fortress Press, 1975) pp. 101–14.

Simon is attacked by Peter.[9] The echoes of Gal. 1.12, 16, 18 and 2.5 and 11 are fairly evident. Peter denies that the teaching of Jesus comes through a vision: 'He who has a vision should recognize that this is the work of a wicked demon.' In contrast Peter received the truth through discernment:

In this way was the Son revealed to me also by the Father. Wherefore I know the power of revelation ... And if our Jesus appeared to you also and became known in a vision and met you as angry with an enemy, yet he has spoken only through visions and dreams or through external revelations ... How can he have appeared to you if you desire the opposite of what you have learned? ... do not contend with me, who am his confidant; for you have in hostility withstood me, who am a firm rock, the foundation stone of the church ... And if you call me 'condemned', then you accuse God, who revealed Christ to me, and disparage him who called me blessed on account of the revelation. But if you really desire to co-operate with the truth, then learn first from us what we have learned from him and, as a learner of the truth, become a fellow worker with us.

Evidently the hostility provoked by Paul's stand on circumcision and at Antioch, and not least as that stand was recorded and defended in Galatians itself, remained a bone permanently stuck in the throat of many Jewish Christians.

Not surprisingly, given the influence of Paul's account of the Antioch incident on both wings of developing Christianity, the representatives of what was becoming the great Church of the middle ground found it necessary to engage also with the problems posed by Galatians for a more positive appraisal of the relations between the two great apostles. Some of these were fairly desperate: Irenaeus and Tertullian argued that the negative should be omitted in 2.5 and the text read, 'to them we yielded submission for a time', thus supporting the claim that Paul did after all submit to the authority of the Jerusalem apostles; Clement of Alexandria suggested that the Cephas of 2.11 was another Cephas, not Peter; and others maintained that the incident itself was a put-up job, staged by Peter and Paul to make the refutation of the judaizers more effective. The general deduction was that Peter accepted Paul's rebuke, that

---

[9] The extracts can be conveniently consulted in Betz, *Galatians* pp. 331–3.

table-fellowship between Christian Jew and Christian Gentile was resumed on the former conditions, and thus the truth of the gospel was maintained by all the Christian leadership, unchanged and strengthened.[10]

THE MODERN PERIOD

Martin Luther – justification by faith

With the Reformation, Galatians emerged from centuries of relative obscurity and became a major theological force once again. The most significant single work here was Martin Luther's lectures on Galatians (1531), published from students' notes in 1535. It would not be unfair to say that this commentary, with its fully worked out treatment of gospel and law, became as influential for the shaping and promotion of the most distinctive and characteristic notes of Lutheran theology as Galatians itself. Here we can give only a flavour of the extended exposition.[11]

In his introductory comments Luther makes it clear that the theme of Galatians is two kinds of righteousness and the distinction between them, 'the righteousness of the law and the righteousness of Christ', the former characterized as 'active and working righteousness' and the latter as 'passive and received righteousness'. The terms already indicate how Luther understood righteousness from works of the law, as righteousness achieved by human activity and effort ('merit-mongers'). The exposition of the second part of 2.16 begins with this typically vigorous argument:

This is the true mean of becoming a Christian, even to be justified by faith in Jesus Christ, and not by the works of the law. Here we must stand, not upon the wicked gloss of the schoolmen, which say, that faith then justifieth, when charity and good works are joined withal.

---

[10] For a review of the history of interpretation of the Antioch incident see Mussner, *Galater* pp. 146–67; Longenecker, *Galatians* pp. xliii–lii contains notes of other points at which the influence of Galatians on patristic theology is discernible.

[11] J. Dillenberger's *Martin Luther. Selections From His Writings* (Anchor Books; New York: Doubleday, 1961) includes some extensive extracts from the 1575 'Middleton' edition, revised and edited by P. S. Watson (London: James Clarke, 1953).

With this pestilent gloss the sophisters have darkened and corrupted this and other like sentences in Paul, wherein he manifestly attributeth justification to faith only in Christ. But when a man heareth that he ought to believe in Christ, and yet notwithstanding faith justifieth not except it be formed and furnished with charity, by and by he falleth from faith, and thus he thinketh: If faith without charity justifieth not, then is faith in vain and unprofitable, and charity alone justifieth; for except faith be formed and beautified with charity, it is nothing ... Wherefore we must avoid this gloss as a most deadly and devilish poison, and conclude with Paul, that we are justified, not by faith furnished with charity, but by faith only and alone ... We grant that we must teach also good works and charity, but it must be done in time and place, that is to say, when the question is concerning works, and toucheth not this article of justification.

Speaking on 2.19 Luther responds to the old idea of Jerome and others that by works of the law Paul referred only to the ceremonial law:

Here Paul speaketh not of the ceremonial law; for he sacrificed in the Temple, circumcised Timothy, shaved his head at Cenchrea. These things had he not done, if he had been dead to the ceremonial law, but he speaketh of the whole law. Therefore the whole law, whether it be ceremonial or moral, to a Christian is utterly abrogate, for he is dead unto it. Not that the law is utterly taken away: nay, it remaineth, liveth, and reigneth still in the wicked. But a godly man is dead unto the law like he is dead unto sin, the devil, death, and hell: which notwithstanding do still remain, and the world with all the wicked shall still abide in them. Wherefore when the sophister understandeth that the ceremonial law only is abolished, understand thou, that Paul and every Christian is dead to the whole law, and yet the law remaineth still ... He that liveth to the law, that is, seeketh to be justified by the works of the law, is and remaineth a sinner: therefore he is dead and condemned. For the law cannot justify and save him, but accuseth, terrifieth, and killeth him. Therefore to live unto the law is to die unto God: and contrariwise, to die to the law is to live unto God ... Now, to live unto God, is to be justified by grace or by faith for Christ's sake, without the law and works.

These extracts are enough to show that Luther had fully grasped Paul's principal thrust on the sufficiency of faith. His own experience had taught him thoroughly that any attempt to add conditions to the acceptability of human beings before

God is a breach and distortion of the essential truth of the gospel. And his restatement of this insight, not least in his lectures on Galatians, lit a torch which has continued to illuminate western Christianity ever since. For many, particularly of the Lutheran tradition, the doctrine of justification by faith as rediscovered and expounded by Luther remains the touchstone of the gospel and the canon within the canon by which authentic Christian theology can be discerned.

The corollary of Luther's restatement, however, was less fortunate. For in understanding 'works of the law' as good works done to achieve righteousness his thinking was beginning to run at a tangent to Paul's. Moreover, in attributing this belief in self-achieved righteousness to the Jews of Paul's day he added a further twist to the disparagement of Judaism which was not uncommon in his own day. And, not least, in interpreting the whole theology of justification by faith in terms of his own individual search for a quiet conscience, he lost sight of the whole corporate dimension of Paul's doctrine as a way of asserting that Gentiles could be reckoned wholly acceptable to God without becoming proselytes.[12] The gain which Luther's emphasis has brought to theology is in no doubt and has often been explored. But an interpretation of the theology of Galatians more closely related to the historical situation of the letter itself will want to bring out the other aspects too.

It is important to appreciate that both emphases are rooted in a fundamental assertion of the sufficiency of faith; both protest against any attempt to add or require something more than faith on the human side when computing what makes a person acceptable to God. The difference which became apparent in earlier chapters is that the added factor against which Paul himself was protesting was not individual human effort, but the assumption that ethnic origin and identity is a factor in determining the grace of God and its expression. Ethnic origin and identity is a different way of assessing human worth, but one more fundamental than the question of ability to perform good works. What Paul protested against was even

---

[12] See further my 'The Justice of God. A Renewed Perspective on Justification by Faith', *JTS* 43 (1992) pp. 1–22; and above pp. 75–9.

more insidious – the assumption that the way people are
constituted by birth rules them in or rules them out from
receiving God's grace. Paul's protest was not against a high
regard for righteousness, against dedicated devotion to God's
law. It was rather against the corollary to such devotion: that
failure to share in that devotion meant exclusion from the life of
the world to come, and that the majority of peoples of the
world were in principle so excluded.

The gain of Luther's individualistic restatement of Paul's
doctrine of justification by faith cannot be too highly valued,
but it also cannot wholly compensate for the loss of the fully
rounded doctrine which we find in Galatians when read within
its historical context.

J. B. Lightfoot – Christianity and Judaism

Three hundred years later Galatians once again became the
focus of vigorous controversy. This was the result of the first
critical attempt to reconstruct the beginnings of Christianity.
For F. C. Baur this was best seen in terms of Christianity's
breaking free from Judaism and as marked throughout by the
opposition between the Jewish particularism of Petrine Christianity and the universalism of Pauline Christianity.[13] Not
unnaturally, Galatians with its forthright denunciation of
'judaizers', including its recollection of the confrontation
between Peter and Paul at Antioch, provided an indispensable
foundation for the theory.[14] Equally unsurprising is the fact
that when J. B. Lightfoot, who spent most of his scholarly life
refuting Baur's historical reconstruction, first joined battle on
the subject, it was Galatians to which he turned. As he himself
noted: 'it is felt by both sides that the Epistle to the Galatians is
the true key to the position'.[15]

The debate ran far beyond Galatians, of course, but in his

---

[13] For a fuller description see my *The Partings of the Ways between Christianity and Judaism*
(London: SCM/Philadelphia: TPI, 1991) ch. 1.

[14] See now A. Wechsler, *Geschichtsbild und Apostelstreit. Eine forschungsgeschichtliche und
exegetische Studie über den antiochischen Zwischenfall (Gal. 2.11–14)* (Berlin: de Gruyter,
1991).

[15] Lightfoot, *Galatians* p. 293.

commentary Lightfoot demonstrated the way to deal with such historical questions – by rigorous historical analysis of the language and context of the key texts – and thus sharpened the issues posed by Baur, while at the same time effectively demolishing the major pillars of Baur's own reconstruction. What resulted was itself epochal – the first of a new genre of commentaries, the first fruits of historical criticism in commentary form, gleaned by one who had a mastery of the ancient texts rarely equalled then or since, a superb sense of proportion and a concise and compelling style. Lightfoot's *Galatians* has provided a model for commentators ever since, and, nearly 130 years since it was first penned, it is still regularly consulted when later commentaries are forgotten.[16]

The debate initiated by Baur on Christianity's emergence from first-century Judaism faded from view for most of the past century, but has re-emerged with renewed vigour in the last fifteen years, particularly in the wake of Sanders' *Paul and Palestinian Judaism*.[17] And once again, as might be expected, Galatians is in the forefront of the debate, posing as it does such questions as the following. Does Paul in Gal. 1.15–16 describe a 'conversion' from Judaism, a conversion within 'Judaism', or a prophetic commissioning (within Israel's prophetic tradition)? Did his doctrines of justification by faith, of the significance of Christ's death, and of the law emerge directly and immediately from his encounter on the Damascus road? What was achieved at the Jerusalem consultation and what was at stake both in Antioch and in Galatia? By 'works of the law' did Paul denote good works, in terms asserted by Luther, or the 'covenantal nomism' by which the devout Jew lived within the covenant in obedience to its law? Was Paul's attitude to the law wholly negative or just inconsistent? What is the gospel? How are the sufficiency of faith and the importance of experience to be maintained? What kind of ethical programme is envisaged and made possible by 'walking by the Spirit'? How is Christian freedom best safeguarded and expressed? How fundamental to

---

[16] For an assessment and appreciation of Lightfoot see *The Lightfoot Centenary Lectures*, ed. J. D. G. Dunn, *Durham University Journal* special issue (1992).

[17] London: SCM, 1977; see above p. 76 n. 21.

Christianity is a 'realized' eschatological perspective (and what can it mean for today)? And, not least, how do the stories of Israel and of Jesus Christ interrelate, who are 'the Israel of God', and how should contemporary Christianity and Judaism understand and mutually relate to their shared historic beginnings? Such questions should not be dismissed as merely historical curiosities. To do so simply betrays a lack of awareness of how such issues have shaped and continue to shape Christianity until today, and of how Paul's own theological wrestling can still be a resource for contemporary discussion of their modern counterparts.

Paul evidently had his own strong views on these matters and provides a most striking example of one attempting to maintain the continuity of shared conviction and experience with his own compelling sense that the integrity of the gospel was at stake and its liberating, enabling power in danger of being lost. The fact that his voice was heard and his vision sustained, at least to the extent that Galatians is part of the canon of Christian scripture, should both encourage those who find themselves lone voices in current theological debates, and remind them that the assessment of theological value may be a long-term affair. We have attempted above to sketch out the emphases that Paul felt so strongly about, and their mutual interrelation. But that attempt is itself only part of the current debate about what Paul meant and about how to appropriate what he means for today. That debate itself is continuing testimony to the theological fascination and spiritual potency of his letter to the Galatians.

Further reading

COMMENTARIES OF GALATIANS

Betz, H. D. *Galatians* (Hermeneia; Philadelphia: Fortress Press, 1979)
A pioneer analysis of rhetorical criticism; very strong on Greco-Roman context of language and usage.

Bruce, F. F. *Commentary on Galatians* (NIGTC; Exeter: Paternoster, 1982)
The climax of a life's scholarship on territory often traversed earlier.

Burton, E. de W. *The Epistle to the Galatians* (ICC; Edinburgh: T. & T. Clark, 1921)
Specializes in careful word studies – a forerunner of *TDNT*.

Dunn, J. D. G. *Galatians* (London: A. & C. Black, 1993)
The commentary which accompanies the present study; the first to take detailed account of 'the new perspective on Paul'.

Fung, R. Y. K. *The Epistle to the Galatians* (Grand Rapids: Eerdmans, 1988)
Conservative but well informed.

Lightfoot, J. B. *Saint Paul's Epistle to the Galatians* (London: Macmillan, 1865, 10th edn 1890)
A classic commentary which pioneered the modern commentary, still of considerable value.

Longenecker, R. N. *Galatians* (WBC 41; Dallas: Word, 1990)
Particularly valuable for its analysis of the epistolary structure and detailed study of particular aspects.

For those who can read German the most valuable commentaries are those of U. Borse (Regensburger Neues Testament, 1984), F. Mussner (HTKNT 3rd edn 1977), J. Rohde (Theologischer Handkommentar zum Neuen Testament, 1989) and H. Schlier (KEK 4th edn 1965)

SPECIAL STUDIES

Barclay, J. *Obeying the Truth. A Study of Paul's Ethics in Galatians* (Edinburgh: T. & T. Clark, 1988)
A very welcome treatment of the letter focusing on its last two chapters.

Barrett, C. K. *Freedom and Obligation. A Study of the Epistle to the Galatians* (London: SPCK, 1985)
The greatest modern British NT commentator never wrote a commentary on Galatians, but this is more than an appetite whetter.

Bassler, J. M. ed., *Pauline Theology. Volume I: Thessalonians, Philippians, Galatians, Philemon* (Minneapolis: Fortress Press, 1991)
Essays from the ongoing SBL seminar on the theology of the Pauline letters.

Cosgrove, C. H. *The Cross and the Spirit. A Study in the Argument and Theology of Galatians* (Macon, Georgia: Mercer University Press, 1988)
Recognizes the central importance of 3.1–5 for understanding the letter.

Drane, J. W. *Paul, Libertine or Legalist? A Study in the Theology of the Major Pauline Epistles* (London: SPCK, 1975)
Sees Galatians as giving too much scope for a libertine reaction against the law.

Dunn, J. D. G. *Jesus, Paul and the Law. Studies in Mark and Galatians* (London: SPCK/Louisville: Westminster, 1990)
Detailed studies which underlie the above exposition.
The Partings of the Ways between Christianity and Judaism and their Significance for the Character of Christianity (London: SCM/ Philadelphia: TPI, 1991)
The larger canvas within which Galatians should be set.

Ebeling, G. *The Truth of the Gospel. An Exposition of Galatians* (Philadelphia: Fortress Press, 1985)
Vintage Lutheran exposition by vintage Lutheran.

Gaston, L. *Paul and the Torah* (Vancouver: University of British Columbia Press, 1987)
Original lines of exegesis, including essays on Galatians.

Hansen, G. W. *Abraham in Galatians. Epistolary and Rhetorical Contexts* (JSNTS 29; Sheffield Academic, 1989)
A more than useful application of epistolary and rhetorical analysis to clarify the force of the Abraham argument in ch. 3 and the allegory in ch. 4.

Hays, R. B. *The Faith of Jesus Christ. An Investigation of the Narrative*

Substructure of Galatians 3.1–4.11 (SBLDS 56; Chico: Scholars Press, 1983)

An influential treatment using narrative theory effectively and arguing that *pistis Christou* means 'the faith of Christ' rather than 'faith in Christ'.

Howard, G. *Paul: Crisis in Galatia. A Study in Early Christian Theology* (SNTSMS 35; Cambridge University Press, 1979, 2nd edn 1990)

Full of sharp exegetical insight, arguing *inter alia* that the agitators in Galatia thought that Paul also preached circumcision.

Hübner, H. *Law in Paul's Thought* (Edinburgh: T. & T. Clark 1984)

Sees a major shift in Paul's theology of the law between Galatians and Romans.

Lull, D. J. *The Spirit in Galatia. Paul's Interpretation of* Pneuma *as Divine Power* (SBLDS 49; Chico: Scholars Press, 1980)

Brings out the importance of the Spirit in Galatians.

Sanders, E. P. *Paul, the Law, and the Jewish People* (Philadelphia: Fortress Press, 1983)

A more satisfactory development of the final section of his influential *Paul and Palestinian Judaism* on Paul's theology, with major sections on Galatians.

Thielman, F. *From Plight to Solution: A Jewish Framework for Understanding Paul's View of the Law in Galatians and Romans* (SNT 62; Leiden: Brill, 1989)

An effective attempt to rebut Sanders' influential thesis that Paul's theology worked from solution to plight.

Watson, F. *Paul, Judaism and the Gentiles. A Sociological Approach* (SNTSMS 56; Cambridge University Press, 1086)

Argues that Paul wanted to encourage his churches to make a clean break with the Jewish community.

Wright, N. T. *The Climax of the Covenant. Christ and the Law in Pauline Theology* (Edinburgh: T. & T. Clark, 1991)

Original lines of exegesis, including two essays on Galatians.

Index of references

OTHER CHRISTIAN WRITINGS

OTHER ANCIENT WRITINGS

Index of names

Index of subjects

Palms Presbyterian Church
Adult Library
3410 South Third Street
Jacksonville Beach, FL 32250